In *Looking for God in Harry Potter*, John Granger doesn't just offer apologies for Christians to sneak around and read Harry Potter books behind the barn. Instead, he boldly claims these books for Christ, showing example after example of the Christian message they proclaim. John leads all readers, whether Christian or not, to delight in the richness of the books, while at the same time revealing the reason why the stories resonate with so many people: because the Harry Potter stories, filled with love and redemption and the struggle to uphold what is good and right, tell the stories of our own longings and hopes. *Looking for God in Harry Potter* is a r   ;ardless of their faith.

STEVE VANDER ARK
Editor, *The Harry Potter Lexicon*

Are the Harry Potter books wort   es, and then some, argues John Granger. '   sɪɪuɪɪ ɪɪarry Potter are denying themselves a serious intellectual and scholarly challenge. Christian thinkers who eschew the Potter series because they find it grates on their theology miss the opportunity to take up once again the daunting question of evil. Wisdom often comes through the eyes and thoughts of children and, in this case, "children's books."

JEAN BETHKE ELSHTAIN
Professor of Social and Political Ethics, The University of Chicago
Author of *Just War Against Terror: The Burden of American Power in a Violent World*

John Granger's thorough knowledge of classical literature, combined with a beguiling writing style, make this study of Harry Potter's hidden themes not only enjoyable but persuasive. Parents will find here a useful tool, and any Christian curious about Harry will find much to think about.

FREDERICA MATHEWES-GREEN
Columnist for Beliefnet.com and author of *The Illumined Heart: The Ancient Christian Path of Transformation*

John Granger calls upon his gifts as a classicist, a student of Scripture and Christian literature, a teacher, a parent, and a detective to answer the question, Why are the Harry Potter books so popular? He develops a thorough case that the Harry Potter books are essentially Christian fantasy, and their popularity can be attributed to human longing for the Christian truths that hide just beneath the surface of the stories. Mr. Granger presents a preponderance of evidence from the text itself, translates advanced literary concepts with ease, and addresses sensitive issues with forthrightness and clarity. Christians who love the Harry Potter books will love them more; Christians who oppose them will have a lot to think about.

CARRIE BIRMINGHAM, PH.D.
Pepperdine University

John Granger has emerged in recent years as one of the most important voices in the literature concerning J. K. Rowling's Harry Potter series. *Looking for God in*

Harry Potter offers Granger at his most accessible and compelling. His careful analysis provides an exceptional guide to the content and meaning of the Harry Potter novels, as well as practical suggestions on how to approach the books in a meaningful way with children. Those who know and love the Harry Potter series will find that this volume adds a new dimension to their understanding and reading enjoyment. Those who are new to or undecided about the series will gain a great appreciation for what Rowling accomplishes in her novels and for the larger religious tradition that informs her stories. Granger writes with clarity and conviction, and his work is both a joy and an education for the reader. All of those interested in the ways that fiction and faith intersect owe it to themselves to read this book.

AMY H. STURGIS, PH.D.
Liberal Studies Program, Belmont University
Author of various books and articles, including "Harry Potter Is a Hobbit: Rowling's Hogwarts, Tolkien's Fairy-Stories, and the Questions of Readership"

No one puts the case for Harry Potter better than John Granger. This book is full of wisdom and insight. . . . The Potter books are much deeper, and a great deal more wholesome, than the critics realize. If Granger is right, J. K. Rowling is writing in the same tradition as the Inklings. Probably millions of Rowling fans knew it all along, but even longtime readers of Harry Potter will find their appreciation deepened by this eye-opening analysis.

STRATFORD CALDECOTT
Author of *Secret Fire: The Spiritual Vision of J. R. R. Tolkien*

John Granger says a "Great Book" must do three things: (1) ask the big questions about life, (2) answer the questions correctly (in harmony with Christian tradition), and (3) support the answers artistically. According to these guidelines, the Harry Potter books can be celebrated as great fiction. Granger's engaging application of literature, language, and the logic of Christian belief in his book *Looking for God in Harry Potter* may likewise be celebrated as great commentary. Readers will discover in these chapters the essential truth of J. K. Rowling's fictional world—that Love conquers all, even death!

ROBERT TREXLER
Editor, *CSL: The Bulletin of the New York C. S. Lewis Society*

Joanne Rowling is the greatest international "smuggler" in history. She is smuggling thousands of pages of Christian theology into the hearts and minds of millions of people, both young and old. John Granger's book leaves no doubt whatsoever that this is the case. Will Ms. Rowling be unhappy that John has let the cat out of the bag?

DON HOLMES
Retired Christian bookstore owner and distributor

LOOKING FOR GOD IN Harry Potter

JOHN GRANGER

SALTRIVER

AN IMPRINT OF
TYNDALE HOUSE PUBLISHERS, INC.

Visit Tyndale's exciting Web site at www.tyndale.com

TYNDALE is a registered trademark of Tyndale House Publishers, Inc.

SaltRiver and the SaltRiver logo are registered trademarks of Tyndale House Publishers, Inc.

Looking for God in Harry Potter

Designed by Luke Daab

Unless otherwise indicated, all Scripture quotations are taken from the *Holy Bible*, New International Version®. NIV®. Copyright © 1973, 1978, 1984 by International Bible Society. Used by permission of Zondervan Publishing House. All rights reserved.

Scripture quotations marked KJV are taken from the *Holy Bible*, King James Version.

Library of Congress Cataloging-in-Publication Data

Granger, John, date.
    Looking for God in Harry Potter / John Granger.
      p. cm.
    Includes bibliographical references.
    ISBN-13: 978-1-4143-0091-7 (hc)
    ISBN-10: 1-4143-0091-3 (hc)
    ISBN-13: 978-1-4143-0634-6 (sc)
    ISBN-10: 1-4143-0634-2 (sc)
    1. Rowling, J. K.—Characters—Harry Potter. 2. Religion and literature—England—History—20th century. 3. Children's stories, English—History and criticism. 4. Religious fiction, English—History and criticism. 5. Fantasy fiction, English—History and criticism. 6. Potter, Harry (Fictitious character) 7. Rowling, J. K.—Religion. 8. Religion in literature. 9. God in literature. I. Title.
    PR6068.O93Z678 2004
    823'.914—dc22   2004004666

Printed in the United States of America.

11   10   09   08   07   06
7   6   5   4   3   2   1

ACKNOWLEDGMENTS

So many people have contributed to this book that only the mistakes are my own; no doubt these errors are substantial enough that I am justified in putting my name on the cover. I have only a short space to thank a large number of friends and will certainly leave out several people who helped me a great deal. They know me well enough to understand this is distraction, not ill will. I ask their forgiveness in advance for this necessarily incomplete list. As nothing I write can express my appreciation, I will leave the list as nothing more than names.

I will always be grateful to the people who have supported me from the beginning of my thinking about Harry Potter and who encouraged me by their excitement and questions about the ideas. Without them, I could not have found the courage to speak and write out my thoughts: Tiffany Harris, Megan O'Loughlin, Karen Plank, Frederica Mathewes-Green, Robert Trexler, Stephen and Colleen Schumacher, Doug Trainer, Beth de Jarnette, Jean Tarascio, Jim Nyby, Richard Watson, James Devine, Arthur Remillard, James Wetmore, and Stratford Caldecott. A special thanks to Stephen, Bob, "Dim," Don, and Doug for their kindness and support last year.

The friends I have made since becoming that most peculiar beast, a "Harry Potter authority," are the best part of the experience. I have made friends (via the Internet) on six continents and archipelagos, worked with many others, and learned more than I should admit from all of them. Their reviews of my first book, e-mail, letters, corrections, ideas, high fives, polite rebukes, and questions have whetted my stone and provided whatever edge my arguments have. Thank you for the love, friendship, and kindness (and please forgive me if I didn't footnote all your ideas in the book!): Don Holmes, Terry Mattingly, Linda McCabe, Penny Linsenmayer, Cathy Strachan-Sherrow, Robert Henderson, Steve Vander Ark, Anne Graves, Carrie Birmingham, Amy Sturgis, Scott Moore, Hans Rieuwers, Alison Williams, Timothy Collinson, Ray Serebrin, Stanton Lindgren, Jonathan King, Xavier Basora, Tara McElhone, Julianne Wiley, LeighAnna Flagg, Magdelena Kurowska, Claire Matson, Kitty Serling, Patrick Barnes, James Calvert, Mark Cameron, Ken McCormick, Donna Farley, Seth York, Fr. Angelo Mary Geiger, Marie Little, Dan Kees, Ann Laurel Nickel (and her dad), Janice Hill, Athanasios Spine, Jean Bethke Elshtain, Richard Abanes, Philip Nel, Connie Neal, Mark Shea, Phina Pipia, Amy Welborn, Emily Stimpson, David Mills, William Bader, Fr. Christopher Metropulos, Brenda Gurung, Jody Kakacek, Vincent Kling, Pat Henderson, Sandra Miesel, Janet Batchler, and Regina Doman.

My family worships at The Church of the Dormition in Port Townsend, Washington, on the Olympic Peninsula. I am grateful for the fellowship, prayers, and support of our church community, and for the leadership of our bishops in California, The Most Reverend Chrysostomos and The Right Reverend Auxentios; our priests here, Fr. Gabriel Lee and Fr. Joseph Miller; and our summertime Deacon, Fr. George Chee.

I confess to some concern about publishing with a big publishing house. I was afraid that the new guy would be lost in the big stable of successful authors. Janis Harris and Lisa Jackson at Tyndale have almost convinced me, because of their personal attention to this project and rapid responses to any and all of my requests, that I am, in fact, the only author at Tyndale and this their second most important book (*The Living Bible* taking first place). I am glad that you, kind reader, will never know how much better a book this is because of Lisa's many changes and editorial suggestions.

If there is one person responsible for the book you are reading, though, it is Kathryn Helmers of Helmers Literary Services. She is supposed to be my literary agent, but in fact, she is more like a human Swiss Army knife. In addition to finding a publisher and negotiating contracts, Kathryn edits, cheerleads, strikes deals, bails water, corrects bad attitudes, breaks impasses, heals the sick, and forcefully presents "the position of the author" (oftentimes to the confused author). Thank you, Kathy, for your professional work on this project and for babysitting your rookie author through the process.

Last on this list but first in my heart is my family. Thank you, Hannah, Sarah, Sophia, Methodios, Anastasia, Timothy, and Zossima for your patience and forgiveness with Daddy on the days he locked himself in his office to write this book. Believe me, I would rather have been reading Pyle's *King Arthur* or running in the park across the street. Thank you, Mary, for covering all the homeschooling and financial bases while I wrote this book and for reading *King Arthur*, playing in the park, and keeping the clan together. You're beautiful and I love you.

John Granger

Irondale, Washington
Clean Monday, 2004
john@hogwartsprofessor.com

This book is dedicated to my father, Albert Lawrence Granger, and my mother, Mary Elizabeth Granger, in gratitude for my education and spiritual formation, and for their support and love through "thick and thin."

PUBLISHER'S PREFACE

Dear Reader,

Some may wonder why a publisher of distinctly Christian books would publish a book about the Harry Potter series, which, while phenomenally successful, has been criticized by some groups within the Christian community. The answer is really quite simple.

Millions of young people are reading the Harry Potter books, providing parents with a wonderful opportunity to use stories their children love to read to start discussions with them about Christian ideas and values—and about how to evaluate the worldview embedded in any piece of literature. We hope Looking for God in Harry Potter will serve as a catalyst for such discussions and as a bridge to growth in faith and spiritual understanding.

The Publisher

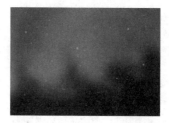

TABLE OF CONTENTS

INTRODUCTION

A Parental Shift from Alarm to Approval

Doubtless you have your own story about the first time you heard of Harry Potter or read a Harry Potter novel. My story, as it reflects the perspective and consequent insights that became this book, is perhaps the fitting way to introduce *Looking for God in Harry Potter.*

I am what reporters without fail call a "traditional Christian." Given that they use this description for Christian believers ranging from snake handlers in Appalachia to Tridentine Mass Roman Catholics, the phrase is robbed of much meaning. But as I fall somewhere between the ends of that spectrum (near the *Mere Christianity* of C. S. Lewis), I can accept the tag. My wife and I have seven children, and we consider it our chief responsibility to raise our children in the context of our faith so they can live fully human lives. Without being paranoid or over-sheltering, we have decided that for our family that means church attendance and family prayers, as well as homeschooling and living without television. Mary and I are also pretty careful about what books we choose to read to the children or what titles we allow them to read. Harry Potter, consequently, was not welcome in my home when I first heard about him.

My concern was less about scaring my children than it was about exposing them to occult elements and forces. I grew up in a time when Dungeons and Dragons was the rage, and I knew a few people whose lives turned around the game for years (and in anything but a healthy way). I also have convictions that, just as there are good spiritual beings, there are harmful spirits as well. Pretending there is no devil is as naive and perhaps as dangerous, if not more so, than seeing demons behind every door. Not being gifted with discernment of spirits, I choose to avoid exposure to anything hinting of the supernatural that is not from a traditional, revealed spiritual path. I observe this simple rule when I buy books for myself as well as when I choose books for my children. This to me is common sense; if it's censorship of a kind, I have to think it's a healthy discrimination—something like reading labels at the grocery store to see if there's a lot of junk in the food.

You should know that because I don't watch television, it's as if I live on one of the moons orbiting the Planet Zeno. I did not hear of Harry Potter until a few months before the fourth volume, *Harry Potter and the Goblet of Fire,* was published. A woman who worked at a natural foods store where I shopped told me about the books and recommended them to me with some enthusiasm. This friend probably would not be described as a "traditional Christian" by most reporters. With her twiggy frame, razor-cut multicolored (mostly orange) hair, tattoos on her neck and ankle, and several facial piercings, Tiffany didn't look like someone you'd expect to meet at a Baptist church picnic. She told me in a conversation over lunch about "these great books about a boy wizard" that I simply *had* to read to my children.

Now, remember, I am almost media-free. What this meant at that time was that I was not only unaware of Harry's existence, I also knew nothing about the controversy involving Christian objections to the Harry Potter books. Looking at Tiffany, though, I didn't think I needed guidance from a children's pastor or Focus on the Family; I assumed my friend was something of a Wiccan or goddess worshipper and made a mental note to keep clear of anything to do with Harry Potter.

But this was not to be. My oldest daughter, then eleven, was given a paperback copy of *Harry Potter and the Sorcerer's Stone* by our pediatrician, who happens to be a thoughtful mother of four children and an evangelical Christian to boot. Now that Harry was in my house, I had to figure out what to do with him. I elected to read the book Hannah had been given, if only to explain to my daughter why she wasn't allowed to read it. I wanted to be able to point to specific passages so she could see for herself why we don't read such trash, however popular it may be.

You can guess the rest of the story, I suppose. I read through the night and, ashamed of my judging a book by its readers, bought the other two books then available early the next morning (and apologized to my friend Tiffany!). I began reading the books to my younger children that night and encouraged—nigh on "required"—that the older kids read them.

I tell my story here for a couple of reasons. First, I hope you will remember that red-flag caution was my first response to Harry Potter as a parent and a reader. I am a great admirer of the Harry Potter books and still maintain that caution in book selection is not ignorance or closed-mindedness. Those who are responsible for the shaping of young minds and hearts *should* be properly careful about what books their charges read in the same way they should be discriminating about what they eat for snacks or what they watch on the television (if they choose to watch it at all). Only the careless or fools equate such prudence with prejudice.

I tell my story, too, in order to begin explaining what is different about *Looking for God in Harry Potter*, namely, the perspective and background I have in reading them. The analyses in this book spring from the same source as my switch from "Harry-resistant" to "Harry-embracing," even "Harry-enthusiastic": my classical education and love of the so-called Great Books.

By a few providential circumstances, I was able to study Latin and Greek in high school (though I was no Hermione, believe me, despite our shared surname). I went to a college that is famous for requiring its students to read the Great Books, or at least large parts of the Western canon. I think now it was more pretension than anything else that made me major in Latin and Greek there, but for whatever reason, I spent a good part of my youth reading Cicero, Virgil, and Aquinas in Latin and Homer, Plato, and Sophocles in Greek.

So what? Well, besides meaning I can translate the magic spells used in Harry Potter (most of which are in Latin), my background is very similar to that of Joanne Rowling, author of the Harry Potter books. Her intellectual pedigree is, in fact, much better than mine.

Rowling was at the top of her class in secondary school, passed A-level exams in French, German, and English, and at the University of Exeter, continued her studies in French and Classical Languages. This is the equivalent of graduating from a prestigious American liberal arts college, say, Middlebury or Wesleyan, with a classical and modern education. She is familiar and fluent with the languages, philosophy, and literature of the classical and medieval worlds. Her books reflect an understanding of the truths of Plato, Aristotle, Augustine, and Aquinas because she has read these greats—and read them as attentively as reading them in the original languages requires.

Rowling and I also enjoy the same taste in English and world fiction. She has expressed in hundreds of interviews (in which she is unfailingly asked about her favorite books and authors) that she loves Charles Dickens and Jane Austen, whose *Emma* is her favorite title. She has said, too, that she is a great admirer of C. S. Lewis, to the point of being physically incapable of being in the same room with a Narnia novel and not sitting down to read it.[1] Her Harry Potter novels, not surprisingly, are filled with allusions to these authors, as well as to William Shakespeare, Leo Tolstoy, Franz Kafka, George Orwell, J. R. R. Tolkien, and Fyodor Dostoyevsky. The themes she explores, the structures of the books, the symbols she uses, even the names of her Harry Potter characters come from (as she likes to say) the "compost heap" in her mind of all the books she has read and loved.[2]

My compost heap of books read and loved is a lot smaller than Rowling's, but it has enough common elements that it smells the same. Reading the first of her Harry Potter books, I was astonished by the range and depth of her story, as well as by its power and profundity. Because I share in several important ways the perspective and background of the author, I was able to understand what makes these books different and better than almost everything being written today. Consequently, I was embarrassed by my ignorance when I learned how popular the books were around the world when I finally read them, but "Potter-mania" was not a surprising or confusing phenomenon. *Of course people everywhere love these books,* I thought. *These stories resonate with the Great Story for which we all are designed.*

What did take me aback was finding out that many segments of the Christian community hated the books. As a Christian daddy, I understood why parents and pastors would be cautious about books involving magic, but having read the books, I had a hard time finding anything but delight in them. *Christians, of all people, should be celebrating the Harry Potter novels and the attendant Potter-mania.* The Potter books are the most edifying works of fiction written in many years, as any classicist, medievalist, or lover of traditional English plays and novels might tell you.

The problem was that these readers and experts weren't telling anybody this. Maybe they weren't reading Harry Potter, or they weren't reading the books closely. Perhaps they thought the work of sharing what Harry Potter is about was beneath them—whatever the reason, I knew that Harry was horribly misunderstood. When I said at a C. S. Lewis Society meeting that these books were within the tradition of great English writing rather than "occult trash," I was told this was a unique interpretation and was invited to expand my comments into a presentation to that group. Which I did.

One thing led to another, starting with a series of lectures on the Potter novels at the Carnegie Library in Port Townsend. Those talks were filmed for television, and eventually the lectures became *The Hidden Key to Harry Potter* (Zossima Press, 2002).

Seemingly overnight, I became a Harry Potter authority of sorts. Since *The Hidden Key to Harry Potter* was published, I was hired to teach a Harry Potter course for Barnes and Noble University online to students around the world, I have lectured around the United States, I was a featured speaker at the first international conference on the meaning of the Potter books (Nimbus-2003, Orlando, Florida), and I have been interviewed on radio stations from coast to coast. I kept my day job, but it has been a lot of fun talking about these books with Harry's friends and foes alike.

In *Looking for God in Harry Potter*, I state my case for what I see as a profoundly Christian meaning at the core of the series. Because this is a short book dealing only with essentials, I have left out much that might interest fans and much that might interest Harry haters. The book does not include, consequently, speculations about Rowling's Christian orthodoxy, her debts to specific authors, or even much about what might happen in the remaining Harry Potter books. Rowling is a professed Presbyterian (Church of Scotland) and has said in interviews that her faith is a key to understanding her work.[3] Nonetheless, no one but God and her immediate circle knows whether this is true or not, so I stick to her books. As you will see, they speak volumes about the power of the Christian message, even in—perhaps especially in—a profane culture.

My thesis is essentially this: *As images of God designed for life in Christ, all humans naturally resonate with stories that reflect the greatest story ever told—the story of God who became man.* The Harry Potter novels, the best-selling books in publishing history, touch our hearts because they contain themes, imagery, and engaging stories that echo the Great Story we are wired to receive and respond to. *Looking for God in Harry Potter* is a step-by-step walk through these images, themes, and stories to reveal the core of the Harry Potter books and why they are so popular: they address the need (really an innate need akin to our need for physical nourishment) that we have for spiritual nourishment in the form of edifying, imaginative experience of life in Christ.

Because the Harry Potter books serve this purpose, they are excellent vehicles for parents wanting to share the Christian messages of love's victory over death, of our relationship to God the Father through Christ, even of Christ's two natures and singular essence. Based on our reading of Harry Potter, I have had conversations with my children about heaven and hell, the work of the devil in the world, and our hope in Christ.

It has been said that the best books "instruct while delighting." Understanding Rowling's artistry requires that we learn some of the "secret code" of English literature (which until the twentieth century was Christian literature almost without exception) that gives Shakespeare's plays, Robert Browning's poems, and Tolkien's novels their power. *Looking for God in Harry Potter* gives you this hidden key so you can unlock the implicit Christian content of the books and share them with others, from children who are fans to skeptical friends.

Looking for God in Harry Potter has two sections and seventeen chapters. The first section explores the themes, structures, symbols, and even the names of characters and titles of the books, which are rich with Christian significance. The second part is a book-by-book look at these elements in each novel, illuminating their remarkable power and close fidelity to classic literary traditions.

I wrote this book to be read from beginning to end, but I think if I were given a copy I would probably skip to the discussion of my favorite Harry Potter novel first and jump around. I hope you enjoy it, however you choose to read it. If you are a "conservative Christian" like me and you have not read the books (or read only one or part of one before giving up on it), I hope you are encouraged by this book to read or reread the novels. If you are a secret Harry Potter fan who has chosen to stay in the closet for fear of criticism from your faith community, I hope this book empowers you to share how Harry's story harmonizes with God's story. If you are a parent, you will soon be able to share with your children some key points of Christian teaching because you will find them embedded in stories your children love. (I have included an appendix for just this purpose.)

And if you are a Harry Potter fan and not a Christian (maybe one of the many readers who bought the book precisely because so many Christians said that you shouldn't!), my hope is that you will take seriously the possibility that the reason you love these books is because your heart resonates with the deeper story underlying the surface of Harry's stories. This book is not a Christian tract by any means. It is first and last about the meaning of the Harry Potter books. But because Rowling's novels are as popular as they are and have, as you will see, so much implicit and sometimes almost explicit Christian content in them, it would be stranger-than-fiction, something of a believe-it-or-not, if their meaning were not a cause of their popularity.

Because of all the sound and fury in the popular media and coming from many pulpits, it may seem incredible to you that Harry Potter is not contrary to Christian faith but a series of books nurturing faith, especially when their Christian and literary antecedents are understood. Are you ready to test this remarkable world-turned-upside-down hypothesis? Just turn the page and let me tell you why this classicist and Christian dad celebrates the existence of the Harry Potter novels.

1

MAGIC, FANTASY, AND THE CHRISTIAN WORLDVIEW

The "sorcery" in Harry Potter supports biblical teaching, not practice of the occult.

More than any other book of the last fifty years (and perhaps ever), the Harry Potter novels have captured the imagination of the reading public worldwide. Hundreds of millions of copies have been sold to date. However, although the books have been wildly successful, no one as yet has been able to explain their popularity.

The Harry Potter books, in case you too have lived on the Planet Zeno since 1997 or have recently come out of a coma, recount the adventures of an English schoolboy as he advances from grade to grade at Hogwarts School. Hogwarts is no ordinary boarding school, however, and Harry Potter is no typical student—the former is a school for witchcraft and wizardry, and Harry is not only a wizard-in-training, but the target of attack by the worst of evil wizards, Lord Voldemort, and his followers, the Death Eaters. Each book ends with a life-or-death battle against

Voldemort or his servants and enough plot twists to make you dream of saltwater taffy.

I am convinced that the fundamental reason for the astonishing popularity of the Harry Potter novels is their ability to meet a spiritual longing for some experience of the truths of life, love, and death taught by Christianity but denied by secular culture. Human beings are designed for Christ, whether they know it or not. *That the Harry Potter stories "sing along" with the Great Story of Christ is a significant key to understanding their compelling richness.* I take hits from both sides for daring to make such a declaration—from Potter fans who are shocked by the suggestion that they have been reading "Christian" books and from Potter foes who are shocked by the thought that there could be anything "Christian" about books with witches and wizards in them.

As the magical setting of the books has caused the most controversy, I'll start with the setting and several formulas Rowling observes in every book.

MAGICAL SETTING

Some Christians object to Harry Potter because Christian Scripture in many places explicitly forbids occult practice. Though reading about occult practice is not forbidden, these Christians prudently prefer (again in obedience to scriptural admonishments to parents) to protect their children from the books' sympathetic portrayal of occult practice. These Christians believe that such approving and casual exposure to the occult opens the door to occult practice.

Other Christians, whether Harry fans or sideline observers of the controversy, point out that the books are "only stories" and that many stories beloved by Christians (usually the Narnia or Lord of the Rings books are invoked as examples) have portrayed witches and wizards in a positive light.

These two groups square off with compare-and-contrast sessions about Frodo, Aslan, and Harry—arguments as much about taste and prejudice as about substance. Both responses miss the mark, I think. With a clear lack of charity, both camps have made Harry Potter into something of a litmus test—of fidelity to principle on the one hand and of human intelligence on the other.

Given this impasse, I think it pays to note three observations:

1. **Occult practices are universally denounced by major world religions.** Every major religion—Hinduism, Buddhism, Judaism, Christianity, and Islam (not to mention animism)—prohibits invocational sorcery and individual (or unguided) exploration of the spirit world. Why? Calling down occult forces and demons is dangerous, and the world's traditions protect their own by condemning it. Invocational magic and sorcery never work according to human plans (the dark forces always have a different agenda for the sorcerer and his community). Being concerned about the occult is not a silly, parochial Christian concern restricted to "ignorant fundamentalists"; it is a prudent *human* concern evident in the faiths of the whole world.

2. **Scripture itself contains material about occult practices.** The Bible nowhere forbids reading material with occult elements in it. As there are witches, soothsayers, and possessed prophetesses in the Bible (almost all negatively portrayed), it would be more than odd if Holy Writ spoke against itself. If anything, the New Testament slams those who charge the righteous with sorcery (see Matthew 12:24-28 and Mark 9:38-40). I know devout Christians who hate Harry as well as many who love him; both groups read their Bible daily *and* enjoy fantasy stories with occult elements and magic in them—stories as diverse as Shakespeare's

The Tempest, L. Frank Baum's Oz stories, Lewis's Narnia and Ransom novels, and Tolkien's Lord of the Rings trilogy.

3. **Whether or not to read Harry Potter from the logical, human view, then, is a question of whether reading Harry fosters a curiosity in the occult or in a rewarding spiritual life.** Scripture forbids occult practice and tells us to "train a child in the way he should go" (Proverbs 22:6). The much-debated question, then, is not whether we are *allowed* to read these books but whether the depiction of magic in them lays the foundation for future involvement in New Age "spirituality." The issue boils down to this: Does Harry foster an interest in the real world occult, or doesn't he?

Despite initially having forbidden my children to read the Rowling books, reading them myself has convinced me that the magic in Harry Potter is no more likely to encourage real-life witchcraft than time travel in science fiction novels encourages readers to seek passage to previous centuries. Loving families have much to celebrate in these stories and little, if anything, to fear.

I say this without hesitation because the magic in Harry Potter is not "sorcery" or *invocational* magic. In keeping with a long tradition of English fantasy, the magic practiced in the Potter books, by hero and villain alike, is *incantational* magic, a magic that shows—in story form—our human thirst for a reality beyond the physical world around us.

The difference between invocational and incantational magic isn't something we all learned in the womb, so let me explain. *Invocational* means literally "to call in." Magic of this sort is usually referred to as sorcery. Scripture warns that "calling in" demonic principalities and powers for personal power and advantage is dangerously stupid. History books, revealed tradition, and fantasy fiction (think *Dr. Faustus*) that touch on sorcery do so in order to show us that the unbridled pursuit of power and advantage via black magic promises a tragic end. *But there is no invocational sorcery in the Harry Potter books.* Even the most evil wizards do their nasty magic with spells; not one character in any of the six books ever calls in evil spirits. Not once.

The magic by spells and wands in Harry Potter is known as incantational wizardry. *Incantational* means literally "to sing along with" or "to harmonize." To understand how this works, we have to step outside our culture's materialist creed (that everything in existence is quantitative mass or energy) and look at the world upside down, which is to say, God-first.

For some, the distinction between invocational and incantational magic is a new idea. I've been asked how prayer fits. "Isn't prayer invocational? Aren't we calling out to God with this concept— invoking his name—when we pray? How is this 'bad magic'?"

Calling out to God isn't bad magic, of course, and the reason helps to clarify the difference between sorcery and the "good magic" of English literature. It is the difference between the psychic and the spiritual realms.[1]

In a materialistic age such as the one in which we live, the distinction between the psychic and the spiritual is hard to keep straight, though it is an understanding all traditional faiths have in common. We struggle to hold on to this distinction because we have been taught that everything existent is some combination of matter and energy. Everything that's not matter and energy, consequently, is lumped together as "peripheral stuff" or "delusion." It's hard to remember the differences between things thrown together in the garbage can of ideas!

The distinction between the psychic realm and the spiritual

realm is critical. The psychic realm—accessible through the soul and including the powers of the soul, from the emotions and sentiments to the reason and intellect—is home to demonic and angelic created beings and is predominantly a fallen place apart from God. The spiritual realm is "God's place"—the transcendent sphere within and beyond creation and the restrictions of being, time, and space.

Invocational magic is calling upon the fallen residents of the psychic realm. Prayer is the invocation of God's name that we might live deliberately and consciously in his presence within time and space.

Incantational magic in literature—a harmonizing with God's Word—is the story-time version of what a life in prayer makes possible. Invoking the powers of the psychic realm is universally forbidden in both literary and Christian traditions. However, calling on the spiritual realm and pursuing graces from it are the tasks for which human beings are designed. The function of traditional English literature, of which Harry Potter is a part, is to support us in this life.

Christianity—and all revealed traditions—believes creation comes into being by God's creative Word, or his song. As creatures made in the image of God, we can harmonize with God's Word and his will, and in doing so, experience the power of God. The magic and miracles we read about in great literature are merely reflections of God's work in our life. To risk overstating my case, the magic in Harry Potter and other good fantasy fiction harmonizes with the miracles of the saints.

C. S. Lewis paints a picture of the differences between incantational and invocational magic in *Prince Caspian*. As you may recall, Prince Caspian and the Aslan-revering creatures of the forest are under attack from Caspian's uncle. Things turn bad for the white hats, and it seems as if they will be overrun and slaughtered at any moment. Two characters on the good guys' side decide their only hope is magic.

Prince Caspian decides on musical magic. He has a horn that Aslan, the Christlike lion of these books, had given to Queen Susan in ages past to blow in time of need. Caspian blows on this divinely provided instrument in his crisis.[2] By sounding a note in obedience and faith, Caspian harmonizes with the underlying fabric and rules of the Emperor over the Sea, and help promptly and providentially arrives.

Nikabrik the dwarf, in contrast, decides a little sorcery is in order. He finds a hag capable of summoning the dreaded White Witch in the hope that this power-hungry, Aslan-hating witch will help the good guys (in exchange for an opening into Narnia). Needless to say, the musical magicians are scandalized by the dwarf's actions and put an end to the sorcery lickety-split.

In the Narnia stories and other great fantasy fiction, good magic is incantational, and bad magic, which is contrary to Scripture, is invocational. Incantational magic is about harmonizing with God's Word by imitation. Invocational magic is about calling in evil spirits for power or advantage—always a tragic mistake. The magic in Harry Potter is exclusively incantational magic in conformity with both literary tradition and scriptural admonition. Concern that the books might "lay the foundation" for occult practice is misplaced, however well intentioned and understandable, because it fails to recognize that Potter magic is not demonic.

Perhaps you are wondering, If Harry Potter magic is a magic in harmony with the Great Story, why are the bad guys able to use it? Great question.

Just as even the evil people in "real" life are certainly created in God's image, so all the witches and wizards in Potterdom, good and bad, are able to use incantational magic. Evil magical folk choose of their own free will to serve the Dark Lord with their magical faculties just as most of us, sadly, lend a talent or power of our own in unguarded moments to the evil one's cause. As we will see, the organizing structure of the Potter books is a battle between good guys who serve truth, beauty, and virtue and bad guys who lust after power and private gain.

Some fans of Lewis and Tolkien contrast their use of magic with Rowling's, arguing that, unlike the world of Harry Potter, the subcreations of these fantasy writers had no overlap with the real world. They suggest that this blurring of boundaries confuses young minds about what is fiction and what is reality.

But Lewis and Tolkien blurred boundaries with gusto in their stories—as did Homer, Virgil, Dante, and other authors whose works regularly traumatize students in English classes. Certainly the assertion that Middle Earth and Narnia are separate realities is questionable, at best. Middle Earth *is* earth between the Second and Third Ages (we live in the so-called Fourth Age). Narnia overlaps with our world at the beginning and end of each book, and in *The Last Battle* is revealed as a likeness with earth of the heavenly archetype, or Aslan's kingdom. Singling out Rowling here betrays a lack of charity, at least, and perhaps a little reasoning chasing prejudgment.

That the magical world exists inside Muggledom (nonmagical people are called "Muggles" by the witches and wizards in Harry Potter), however, besides being consistent with the best traditions in epic myth and fantasy, parallels the life of Christians in the world. I don't want to belabor this point, but C. S. Lewis described the life of Christians as a life spent "in an enemy occupied country."[3] What he meant is that traditional Christians understand that man is fallen, that he no longer enjoys the ability

to walk and talk with God in the Garden, and that the world is
driven by God-opposing powers. Lewis's Ransom novels illus-
trate this idea.

Christians believe that their resistance to the occupying powers
and their loving service to God qualify them as a peculiar people who
are "in the world" but not "of the world" (John 17:13-16). Though
the church has left the catacombs (except in some Muslim and totali-
tarian countries in which Christians still worship in secret and at risk
of their lives), Christians true to their revelation and tradition understand that they serve a different Lord than the lord of the world.

The magical and secret world inside Muggledom is not cause
for concern so much as it is a parallel to celebrate. I am not offering the magical world as an allegory (shudder) for the church;
Rowling satirizes every institution—media, government, courts,
schools, hospitals, families—and most human foibles in her sub-
creation. But I do think that her secret world within our world
coincides with rather than contradicts the worldview of Christians.

Which brings me full circle. I started by saying that understanding incantational magic requires turning the modern
worldview on its head, putting God first rather than last. I hope
you see that the magic by spells and wands requires that we understand our world as a created world dependent for its existence on
God's creative Word.

We live in a time in which *naturalism*, the belief that all existence
is matter and energy, is the state religion and belief in supernatural
or contra-natural powers is considered delusion. The incantational
magic in Harry Potter, because it requires harmonizing with a
greater magic, undermines faith in this godless worldview. And by
undermining the materialist view of our times, it can even be said
that the books lay the foundation not for occult practices but for
a traditional understanding of the spiritual life.

The magic in Harry Potter is consistent with and even fosters a worldview affirming spiritual realities because

- it is incantational rather than forbidden invocational magic;
- it illustrates the right and wrong uses of power and talents;
- its world inside Muggledom parallels the Christian worldview;
- it reinforces the Christian view of the world as a creation rather than a natural accident devoid of meaning.

Have you heard stories of children being sucked into witches' covens because they want to be like Harry? Reports of rising membership in occult groups since these books were published inevitably turn out to be generated by proselytizing members of these groups. People who track the occult for a living explain that, despite Buffy the Vampire Slayer and Harry Potter, membership in these groups in Europe and the United States is minuscule and has been in decline over the last decade.[4] Your child is far more likely to become a Hare Krishna or member of a Christian cult than a witch or wizard.

And even if children *were* being seduced into the occult because of their desire to do spells, I have to hope this would be understood by thinking people as a shameful, tragic aberration, more indicative of the child's spiritual formation than a danger in the books. The Dungeons and Dragons craze in the sixties and seventies and its attendant occult paraphernalia sprang from an unhealthy fascination and perverse misunderstanding of *The Lord of the Rings,* an epic with clear Christian undertones. If we were to avoid books that could possibly be misunderstood or whose message could be turned on its head, incidents like Jonestown would logically suggest we should not read the Bible.

What about the title of the first book in the Potter series? If there's no sorcery in these books, how come the first book and movie are titled *Harry Potter and the Sorcerer's Stone?* Well, because that isn't the title of the first book. Arthur Levine, under whose imprint the books are published by Scholastic in the United States, changed the title from *Philosopher's Stone* to *Sorcerer's Stone* because he was sure that no American would buy a book with *philosophy* in the title.

An Orthodox Christian bishop has noted that Harry haters "have missed the spiritual forest for the sake of their fixation on the magical imagery of the literary trees."[5] If there is anything tragic in this misunderstanding of Harry Potter by well-intentioned Christians, it is the tragedy of "friendly fire." Just as foot soldiers are sometimes hit by misdirected artillery fire from their own troops, so Harry has been condemned by the side he is serving. Because we mistake fictional magic for sorcery, we misconstrue a well-aimed blow at atheistic naturalism as an invitation to the occult. This only serves to attack a new and valuable ally in the spiritual warfare against our common enemy.[6] If the "magical trees" in Harry Potter are of any help in retaking ground lost to those who would burn down the spiritual forest, then Rowling has done Christian communities everywhere a very good deed.

I receive e-mail from readers almost daily about the "problem" of reading Harry Potter in search of Christian meaning. They insist that the symbols, themes, and meanings of the books are perfectly comprehensible without any reference to an imaginary Christian subtext believers are projecting into the books.

The mistake these readers make when they insist that the symbolism of Harry Potter is not "exclusively" Christian is that they just don't understand a disturbing fact about English literature.

I have friends who teach and write about Saudi Arabia and Arabic culture in general. Their work is not restricted to Islam, certainly, but they wouldn't be experts in their field if they weren't aware of the tremendous influence of the Koran and the Islamic worldview on culture, politics, and everything Arabic. This, I hope, is a no-brainer.

Unfortunately, in a post-Christian era, and one in which universities are in large part overly hostile to religious meanings, the simple, disturbing fact that English literature until the last fifty years was "exclusively" a Christian field escapes people. Christian authors writing for a Christian reading audience—and writing books, plays, and poems that would edify them in their spiritual and workaday lives as Christians—was the rule of English letters until well after the first World War.

If you said this obvious fact out loud, of course, you would be accused of proselytizing or forcing Christian meaning onto texts. I confess that these accusations bewilder me! No one accuses my friends who are Saudi scholars of trying to convert people to Islam because their reports on Middle Eastern current events and trends are heavy on the place of Islam in Arabic culture.

If some Harry fans are uncomfortable because other readers, Christian or not, are interpreting the Potter books in a Christian light, I beg these readers to ask themselves where the problem exists. Reading books within a Christian literary tradition (if *not* for an exclusively Christian audience and *not* in a manner that is overtly Christian in any denominational or parochial sense) invites discussion of the Christian elements of the story and of the tools from the tradition the author uses. Literary alchemy, religious symbolism, and doppelgängers, for instance, don't make much sense outside of the tradition in which these books are written and in which these tools are used.

I have no evangelical cause or agenda here in discussing the Christian content of these books. My only hope is that readers will come to a greater appreciation of these works via the discussion of Harry Potter as traditional English literature, which, again, is an overwhelmingly Christian subject. William Shakespeare's plays and James Joyce's novels are impenetrable outside some appreciation of their spiritual context and the traditions of English literature. Joanne Rowling's stories are no different.

If readers want an exclusively secular view of the books—that is, a reading of them outside of the context and traditions in which they are written—this is probably not their book. English literature (Harry Potter is undeniably root-and-branch English literature) is as Christian as Tibetan culture is Buddhist and Saudi politics is Islamic.

Denying this is not "having a broad mind" but living in a fantasy. Likewise, refusing to see the Christian elements in Harry Potter and insisting it is demonic is not a greater piety or fidelity to the faith; it is just a reflection of not understanding the place of literature in the spiritual life, of not understanding the Christian tradition of English literature, and of not understanding Harry Potter.

This book helps to unfold where Harry Potter fits in this tradition and what a support he can be in the spiritual life.

2
GOD'S ARMY VERSUS THE SERVANTS OF SATAN?

*The Harry Potter novels revolve around
the central conflict of good and evil.*

However fascinating—and to some, distracting and disturbing—the magical backdrop is in Harry Potter, it is only a part of the setting and structure of these stories. A strong case could be made that the magic in these books is one of the less important aspects. Harry isn't an especially accomplished wizard (like the other Gryffindors—except Hermione—he is known for being a bit dull in the classroom) and his magical aptitude isn't what saves him in his battles with the Dark Lord and his minions.

Having argued that the magic in Harry Potter is at the very least consistent with a Christian worldview, let's turn to the other parts of the setting that receive much less media attention than the magic to understand what part of the Great Story each reflects and, in this, to see if they pass a litmus test for conformity to Christian tradition. In a simple list that will be the subject of the next several chapters, these parts include:

- Gryffindor/Slytherin opposition
- The hero's journey
- Alchemical "Great Work"
- Doppelgängers

One of the novelties of the Harry Potter books is that, while each book is an exciting story in itself, there is a larger story that

THE HOUSE OF GRYFFINDOR VERSUS THE HOUSE OF SLYTHERIN

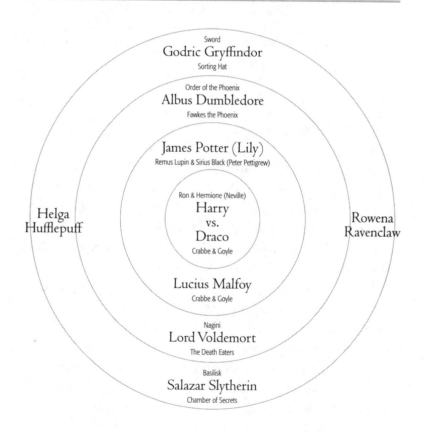

provides the context for these separate adventures. Every book lets the reader in on another part of the puzzle that clarifies the relationships of the major players. The relationship map on page 16 allows the reader to understand at a glance who is on whose side, who opposes whom, and who does not fit neatly into a relationship slot.

If you begin on the map's periphery, you see the founders of Hogwarts School: Salazar Slytherin, Godric Gryffindor, Rowena Ravenclaw, and Helga Hufflepuff. The two defining figures of this quartet are Slytherin and Gryffindor, whose disagreements and characters bleed into the remaining rings. Look for Gryffindor at the top and Syltherin at the bottom, just as their respective dormitory houses are in a tower and a dungeon.

The next ring in, we find Albus Dumbledore and the Order of the Phoenix on the Gryffindor end of the ring and Lord Voldemort and his Death Eaters on the Slytherin end. Voldemort, we learn in *Harry Potter and the Chamber of Secrets,* is Slytherin's heir, and he and his Death Eaters labor to create a world ruled by pure-blooded wizards. Hagrid mentions in *Sorcerer's Stone* that nearly all the wizards who joined with Voldemort were from Slytherin House.

Dumbledore is linked with Gryffindor by artifacts and personal history. He "owns" the Sorting Hat that belonged to Godric Gryffindor and the sword of Godric Gryffindor that Harry pulls from it in *Chamber of Secrets* ("sword-in-hat"—get it?). His office has a griffin door knocker, and more importantly, his life has been spent resisting evil wizards, from the dark wizard Grindewald in 1945 to Lord Voldemort in the present.

The Order of the Phoenix is a counterbalancing group of wizards under Dumbledore's influence (the "old crowd" he tells Sirius Black to bring together at the end of *Goblet of Fire* and whom we meet in *Harry Potter and the Order of the Phoenix*), offsetting the Death Eaters under Lord Voldemort. Dumbledore's glorious pet phoenix, Fawkes, is mirrored in a horrible contrast on the dark side by Voldemort's giant black snake, Nagini.

Moving toward the center, one ring in, we meet the parents of Harry Potter and Draco Malfoy. Lucius Malfoy, a loyal Death Eater and former member of Slytherin House, lines up, of course, on the Slytherin side of the map. I put Crabbe's and Goyle's names here both because we learn that their fathers are Death Eaters and for symmetry with the center ring (where they are inseparable from Draco Malfoy, the son of Lucius and Narcissa).

Harry's father, James, aligns with Gryffindor and Dumbledore. James was in Gryffindor House, lived in Godric's Hollow before his death, and had a close relationship with Dumbledore (close enough that after James died, Dumbledore acted as executor and protector of his son). His opposition to Voldemort, his murderer, is total. Though we learn in *Order of the Phoenix* that James was quite a jerk at fifteen, we know from the great respect shown to him by all but Professor Snape that he was a hero in the war against the Dark Lord.

James's two close friends from school, Remus Lupin and Sirius Black, join him in the ring with parenthetic inclusion of their sidekick and hanger-on, Peter Pettigrew. They balance Crabbe and Goyle and foreshadow Harry's close friends Ron and Hermione—with Neville Longbottom as their hanger-on, similar to Pettigrew (whom he resembles; see *Prisoner of Azkaban*, chapter 11).

In the center ring we find Harry Potter and his great rival, Draco Malfoy. Each lines up ring by generational ring with his respective parents, patron, and house founder. Each has friends who echo in number and character the friends of his parents. Each despises the other and lives for the pleasure of seeing the other fail. Their opposition becomes more open—and violent—with each book.

The major characters, then, fall into place on the Gryffindor/Slytherin axis. The other characters? Hagrid, the Weasleys, and Professor McGonagall are in the Order of the Phoenix, and we have to suspect strongly that Ludo Bagman, the Minister of Magic, and Rita Skeeter (among others) are at least collaborators with Lord Voldemort.

But there are a few question marks. Most importantly, on whose side is Professor Severus Snape? As the master of Slytherin House and an alumnus of the same; an open enemy of Harry Potter, his father, and his father's friends; and a Death Eater with the Dark Mark tattooed on his arm, isn't it obvious? No, not really. Snape haunts Professor Quirrell/Voldemort in *Sorcerer's Stone* and does everything he can to keep him from winning the Stone. He saves Harry's life in the same book and has Dumbledore's trust because he acted as a double agent for the Gryffindor side in the last war with Voldemort. At the end of *Goblet of Fire* and all through *Order of the Phoenix*, Professor Snape returns to Lord Voldemort at Dumbledore's request and at obvious risk of his life. Whose side is he on? He seems to be on his own side, which is to both sides of the map and neither side. Even after he seems to murder Dumbledore in *Half-Blood Prince*, there is good reason to doubt that Snape has shown his true colors. By not being able to place Snape, the map highlights his role as a critical or swing character. Does this Gryffindor/Slytherin opposition have a greater meaning than, say, the struggle between two football teams? Yep.

We need to note that the Slytherins are notoriously vicious and unapologetically focused on getting more power. The Gryffindors, though not incapable of some over-the-top behaviors and reckless-ness, do not torture Muggles for jollies or harass magical folk because they can. The battle between Gryffindor and Slytherin is a battle between good and evil—I will even argue, believe it or not, that it is a reflection of the battle between those who serve Christ and those who serve the evil one.

You may have read critics of the Potter books who assert that Harry's world is morally ambiguous because the white hats need cleaning and the black hats demonstrate sufficient loyalty to one another not to be "jet black." This is silly. As W. H. Auden explained in his defense of Tolkien (yes, he was charged with this type of ambiguity, too), the difference between the good and bad guys in fiction comes down to the choices each makes. Bad guys don't do the wrong thing after struggling with a decision; they almost automatically do what most advances their individual or group advantage without regard for principle. Good guys often are tempted to do the wrong thing—may even *do* the wrong thing—but they either choose the right or repent of their error in light of right and wrong.[1] This is exactly the situation between the Gryffindor white hats and Slytherin black hats. The Gryffindors (most often the lead players: Harry, Ron, and Hermione) choose to do the right thing—usually after some hand-wringing and soul-searching—though doing the right thing will probably mean their death. The Slytherins do the wrong thing without reservation or restraint.

This defining conflict of the series reflects every Christian's battle with the flesh, the world, and the devil. The meanings of the house names, their respective house symbols, and even the title given to Lord Voldemort all point to a parallel with Christianity and the reality of life on earth.

Gryffindor is named for its founder, Godric Gryffindor, whose first name means "godly" or "worshipful." David Colbert, author of *The Magical Worlds of Harry Potter*, tells us that *Gryffindor* is French for "golden griffin" (griffin d'or) and that the griffin is commonly used as a symbol of Christ. Sound like a reach? Hardly. Remember from your fairy tales that a griffin is half lion and half eagle. Lions are considered the kings of the terrestrial animal world, and eagles are considered kings of the sky. An animal that is two-natured, one in essence, and king of heaven and earth? More about symbolism and griffins in chapter 9, but the main point here is that the Gryffindor/Slytherin matchup is a lot bigger than a Cubs/Red Sox slugfest.

Oddly enough (on the surface at least), the house animal on the Gryffindor banners is not a golden griffin but a red lion. This is a clear tip of the hat to Lewis's Aslan, the Christlike lion of the Narnia books, although Lewis didn't invent this symbolism. The red lion as an emblem for Christ is part of traditional and alchemical imagery. The phoenix, sometimes called the "resurrection bird," is also a symbol for Christ and a natural title for Dumbledore's (adult) army in *Order of the Phoenix*. Not enough? Well, how about those Slytherin nasties then? Their connection with the devil is remarkable. Their mascot is a serpent, their founder's name—Salazar Slytherin—is full of hissing serpentine sounds and suggests the motion a snake makes on the ground (slitherin'; see Genesis 3:14), and their leader is the Dark Lord. I don't think this is coincidental. That Voldemort's intimates are called "Death Eaters" is just icing on the cake. (The opposite of Death Eaters is "Life Eaters"—and those who eat the body and blood of God, who is the way, the truth, and the *life*, are Christians.)

Readers familiar with the Bible will recognize Saint Paul's understanding of the world as being fallen (Romans 8:22) and ruled by the devil (2 Corinthians 4:3-4), against whom everything and everyone good is at war—and whose rule and corruption God became man to destroy (Colossians 2:13-15; I Corinthians

15:24-27, 54-57). Christians consciously battle against the principalities and powers (Ephesians 6:12) that subject all men who do not seek to know and resist the devil's thoughts (2 Corinthians 2:11). The central conflict of the Harry Potter books is the antagonism between the descendants of Godric Gryffindor and Salazar Slytherin, a conflict that is consistent with the Christian view of the world as a battleground in the cosmic war between good and evil. The many clues in names and words in the stories point to Gryffindor House as being much like God's army and Slytherin as Satan's servants. We learn more in each book about their battles inside and outside of Hogwarts and the eerie parallels across generations. My hope in this short chapter was to show that this central conflict is both consistent with the Christian worldview (which is to say, an apt description of the world as it really is) and even supportive of this understanding. Given the many clues in names, words, and events that Rowling has given us to point to Gryffindor House as God's army and Slytherin as Satan's servants, we can be assured this is edifying reading for Christians.

As Perry Glazer of Baylor University has written, "Children need more than a set of virtues to emulate, values to choose, rules to obey, or even some higher form of reasoning to attain. They long to be part of a cosmic struggle between good and evil. And that's why children want to read Harry Potter."[2] I would only add, that is why Harry Potter makes excellent reading for children *and* adults; the books both satisfy and support our God-implanted longing to resist evil and serve the good. Can we reasonably ask anything more of our entertainments?

3

THE HERO'S CHRISTLIKE JOURNEY

*Harry's adventures take him
through life, death, and resurrection.*

The Harry Potter books are laid out according to a formula repeated in each story. This formula, used in stories from ancient epics to modern adventure novels, is known by many different names and has been attributed many different meanings.[1] As it is used in the Harry Potter books, the formula is a snapshot of the innate human hope that love conquers death and that we will rise from the dead in a resurrection made possible by and in Christ.

No doubt you find this hard to believe. Let's start, then, just by describing the formula as shown in our second map and seeing what Harry's journey involves. All six books begin and end in the same place and pass a series of landmarks that differ only in details. On the following page is a rough chart of the pattern as it appears in each book:

HARRY'S JOURNEY

	Sorcerer's Stone	Chamber of Secrets	Prisoner of Azkaban	Goblet of Fire	Order of the Phoenix	Half-Blood Prince
START	Privet Drive	Privet Drive	Privet Drive	Privet Drive	Privet Drive	Privet Drive
ESCAPE	Admission letters and Hagrid visit	Flying Ford Anglia	Knight bus	Flu powder	Rescue by Order	Dumbledore pickup
MYSTERY	Stone's seeker and location	Chamber opening and Slytherin heir	Sirius Black's escape	Triwizard Tournament entry	Dreams/ Hogwarts takeover	Draco's suicide mission
CRISIS	Albus leaves	Ginny taken	Ron taken	Third trial	Sirius "kidnapping"	Draco's repair success
DESCENT	Trapdoor	Bathroom chute	Under willow	Graveyard	Ministry of Magic	Into cave, from Tower
COMBAT	Quirrell	Riddle	Black/ Dementors	Voldemort	Death Eaters/ Voldemort	Inferi/ Severus Snape
CHRIST SYMBOLS	Philosopher's Stone	Phoenix	Stag	Phoenix song	Phoenix swallowing death curse	Dumbledore/ Hippogriff
RETURN	Albus, 3 days	Fawkes	Hippogriff	Portkey	Portkey	Alongside apparition
REVELATION	Snape OK, Quirrell = Voldemort	Dobby OK, Riddle = Voldemort	Black OK, Scabbers = Wormtail	Snape a hero, Moody = Death Eater	Dumbledore a human, Voldemort = Dream Weaver	Snape a Death Eater still?
FINISH	Station 9¾	Station 9¾	Station 9¾	Station 9¾	Station 9¾	Dumbledore funeral

Harry's hero journey is a generic picture of each adventure Harry has taken so far.

- He begins at home on Privet Drive with his Muggle family, the Dursleys.
- He escapes to Hogwarts from his living death via the intrusion of extraordinary magic (Hagrid's birthday arrival, the flying Ford Anglia, etc.).

- Harry arrives at Hogwarts to find something mysterious going on.
- With help from Hermione and Ron, Harry tries to solve the mystery, which, inevitably, comes to a crisis demanding his immediate action (with or without his friends).
- He descends into the earth to face this crisis (except in *Goblet of Fire*, in which he portkeys to a graveyard, the surroundings of which have a resonant meaning with the underworld).
- Harry fights Voldemort or a servant of the Dark Lord and triumphs against impossible odds (in books 3, 4, 5, and 6 merely by escaping alive).
- He dies a figurative death, rises from the battlefield with the miraculous help of a Christ figure, and returns to the land of the living.
- Harry learns from Professor Dumbledore that a good guy is really a bad guy and a bad guy is really a good guy (along with the meaning and lesson of his adventure).
- Harry leaves us at Station 9¾ to go home with the Dursleys.

Some friends have told me when I have shown them the second map that they feel cheated somehow. If this were just a mechanical formula, as in TV dramas, disappointment would be warranted. (Remember *The A Team* television program? Same show every week with a different machine at the end to save the day?)

The Harry Potter formula, however, is anything but a scripting cookie cutter. While the story is a partial throwback to the heroes of old (Odysseus, Aeneas, Dante), these stories take quite a different turn. In the ancient and medieval epics, the heroes travel to the underworld to confront death (usually for information), entering and exiting without a trial much greater than the difficulties of the trip and the shock of what they see. Not so in Harry Potter.

Look at the chart again. What happens to Harry underground? Invariably he dies a figurative death.

- In *Sorcerer's Stone*, Harry expires, "[knowing] all was lost, and fell into blackness, down . . . down . . . down . . . " (chapter 17).
- In *Chamber of Secrets*, Harry is poisoned by the basilisk. "Harry slid down the wall. He gripped the fang that was spreading poison through his body and wrenched it out of his arm. But he knew it was too late. . . . 'You're dead, Harry Potter,' said Riddle's voice above him" (chapter 17).
- In *Prisoner of Azkaban*, a dementor lowers his hood to kiss Harry. "A pair of strong, clammy hands suddenly attached themselves around Harry's neck. They were forcing his face upward. . . . He could feel its putrid breath. . . . His mother was screaming in his ears. . . . She was going to be the last thing he ever heard. . . . [When released, Harry] felt the last of his strength leave him, and his head hit the ground" (chapter 20).
- In *Goblet of Fire*, Rowling places Harry's seemingly hopeless battle with the risen Voldemort in a graveyard, so Harry is not only in an almost certain collision course with death, he is also already among the dead (chapters 32–34).
- In *Order of the Phoenix*, Harry is possessed by Voldemort to get Dumbledore to kill the boy. "And then Harry's scar burst open. He knew he was dead: it was pain beyond imagining, pain past endurance" (chapter 36).
- In *Half-Blood Prince*, the Inferi from the cavern lake grab Harry and begin to carry him into the Stygian depths. "He

knew there would be no release, that he would be drowned, and become one more dead guardian of a fragment of Voldemort's shattered soul" (chapter 26).

Not much to recommend the books, though, if the hero merely dies, is there? Harry doesn't just die in these stories, of course; he rises from the dead. And in case you think this is just a "great come-back" rather than a Resurrection reference, please note that Harry never saves himself but is always saved by a symbol of Christ or by love. As you can see from the chart, in *Sorcerer's Stone*, it is his mother's sacrificial love and the Stone; in *Chamber of Secrets*, it is Fawkes the phoenix; in *Prisoner of Azkaban*, it is the white stag Patronus; in *Goblet of Fire*, it is the phoenix song; and in *Order of the Phoenix*, it is Harry's love for Sirius, Ron, and Hermione that defeats the Dark Lord. Both Dumbledore and Buckbeak the hippogriff save Harry as Christ fig-ures in *Half-Blood Prince*. That he rises after three days in *Sorcerer's Stone* is another obvious reference to the Resurrection.

There's a lot more that needs to be said here about death, bereave-ment, and Christian symbols—which I'll get to in chapter 7 and chapter 9—but for now let's leave the hero's journey formula with these two key points:

- The climax of Harry's hero journey invariably turns out to be a strong image of the Christian hope: that death is followed by resurrection in Christ.
- The answer these stories offer to the ultimate human problem—death—is always love or a symbol of Love himself, Jesus Christ.

The point, in brief, is that these books are each built on a struc-ture or skeleton that powerfully drives home a Christian truth the world disregards or denies in its love/hate relationship with death. As the apostle Paul writes in his epistle to the church in Rome, "To be carnally minded is death; but to be spiritually minded is life and peace" (Romans 8:6, KJV). Carnality, or a life in pursuit of personal advantage, is the law of this world—and the magical world as well, it seems. Harry's edifying heroism is his annual journey as an Everyman from this carnality to a dependence on love to overcome death. The beloved disciple tells us that "God is love" (I John 4:8). We see in each Harry Potter novel that it is this love, evident within Harry by the sacrificial love of his mom and in the symbols of Christ around him, that every year raises him up from underground in victory over death. Harry Potter's story is God's plan and our hope.

4

THE ALCHEMY OF
SPIRITUAL GROWTH

*The story cycles are built
on the stages of transformation.*

Maybe you think all this fuss about the hero's journey is wrong-headed. I mean, let's be serious. Going to school in the fall and returning home in the summer—where the destinations are always clearly understood and arrived at—may not seem like much of a journey. But there is another way to look at the Harry Potter stories that is at least as likely as the annual journey: alchemy.

Alchemy, though, is so misunderstood that saying the Harry Potter books are built on alchemical structures and imagery is not much different from saying the books aren't worth reading or that they're dangerous to read.

One of the first lessons in a chemistry class is that chemistry grew out of a kind of medieval voodoo called alchemy, a pseudo-science whose goal was to isolate a philosopher's stone that could turn lead (meaning base metals) into gold and bestow immortality on the alchemist. Alchemy has been called stupid chemistry, fraud, witchcraft, and even a path into the subconscious mind. But for our purposes, alchemy can simply be defined as the transformation of something common into something special. If historians of religion and sacred art are to be believed (most notably, Titus Burckhardt and Mircea Eliade), alchemy was a spiritual path within the great revealed traditions to return fallen man to his Edenic perfection.

Whether they are right or wrong, though, really doesn't matter. Alchemy, whatever it may have been, no longer exists except as a synonym for "magical transformation" and as a resource for artists and authors writing about personal change. Alchemical symbols are a large part of classic English literature. And if we don't understand the idea of alchemy, we can easily miss out on the depth, breadth, and height of plays by Shakespeare, poetry by Donne and Eliot, and the novels of Lewis and Tolkien.[1] Writing in the tradition of writers stretching from Chaucer to Joyce, Rowling uses alchemy in Harry Potter as a metaphor for change and as a resource for powerful imagery.

What is the connection between alchemy and literature that makes alchemical images such useful tools for writers?

I think the connection is probably most clear in drama. Many, if not most, of Shakespeare's plays, in fact, are written on alchemical skeletons and themes.[2] In a proper tragedy, the audience identifies with the hero in his agony and shares in his passion. This identification and shared passion is in effect the same as the experience of the event; the audience experiences catharsis, or "purification," in correspondence with the actors. Shakespeare and Benjamin Jonson, among others, used alchemical imagery and themes because they understood that the work of the theater in human transformation was parallel if not identical to the work of alchemy. The magic of alchemy and stage dramas is that through these external transformations, the alchemist's metals, the audience, and the actors onstage are all purified and transformed from leaden to golden hearts.

Alchemical language and themes are shorthand for transformation. The success of an artist following this tradition is measured by the edification of his audience. By means of traditional methods and symbols, the alchemical artist offers our soul delight and dramatic release through archetypal and purifying experiences.

That may be harder for some of us than believing that alchemy was once a sacred science. If you are like me, you grew up with the idea that reading was entertainment and diversion, and anything but life changing. This idea, really only in currency for the last seventy or eighty years, is a gross misconception. Anthropologists, historians of religion, and professors of literature will all tell you that the rule in traditional cultures, and even in cultures such as ours, is that story, in whatever form, is meant to instruct and change us.

In his book *The Sacred and the Profane*, Eliade argued that entertainments serve a religious function, especially in a profane culture. They remove us from our ego-bound consciousness for an experience or immersion in another world.

Alchemy is a great resource for writers because both the alchemical work and entertainments endeavor to transform the human person. It may not occur to most Christian artists to call their work "alchemical," but that is exactly what films such as *Hoosiers* or *October Sky* and books such as the Left Behind novels and the Lord of the Rings series are designed to accomplish in their audiences: a real-life change triggered by the powerful experience of viewing a film or reading a book.

ALCHEMY IN HARRY POTTER

Where is the alchemy in Harry Potter? It's everywhere from book titles to character transformations. Here are five areas in which alchemical imagery is especially evident in the Harry Potter books.

First, the book titles. The title of the first book is *Harry Potter and the Sorcerer's Stone* (originally *Philosopher's Stone*—creating the philosopher's stone is the goal of alchemy). And it is rumored that Warner Bros. has reserved the title *Harry Potter and the Alchemist's Cell* for the seventh novel.

Second, the alchemical characters. We learn early in the first book that Hogwarts' headmaster and Harry's mentor, Albus Dumbledore, is an alchemist of some renown and a partner of the famous alchemist Nicolas Flamel, a distinction (listed on his chocolate frog trading card) he treasures above all his titles. (Flamel was an actual famous alchemist who lived in fourteenth-century Paris.)

Hermione Granger's name has an obvious alchemical reference in it, too, as do several other names in the books. Hermione is the feminine form of Hermes, who, besides being the Greek messenger god (Mercury), was also the name of the great alchemist Hermes Trismegistos, in whose name countless alchemical works were written through the centuries. Harry's father is named James, the name of the patron saint of alchemists, and his mother is named Lily, a symbol for the second, purifying stage of the alchemical work.

Third, Harry's transformations from lead to gold. The alchemical work is about changing the soul from lead to gold, from failing to virtue; this is evident in the title character's transformations in each book.

In the first, *Sorcerer's Stone*, the orphaned Harry lives in fear of his aunt and uncle, the Dursleys, and without any knowledge or delight in who he is. By the book's end, he shows himself a champion of remarkable courage and daring and has become reconciled both to his parents' death at the hands of the sorcerer Voldemort and to his own destiny as a wizard. In *Chamber of Secrets,* Harry begins the book as a prisoner both of the Dursleys and of his own self-doubts and self-pity. At the heroic finish, he risks his own life to liberate a young girl and vanquish the villain, who is an incarnation of selfishness and self-importance.

Harry blows up his Aunt Marge (like a balloon) because he cannot overlook her slights of his parents at the beginning of *Prisoner of Azkaban.* At the end, he rescues the man who betrayed his parents to Voldemort by offering his own life as a shield to him. He goes from unforgiving judgment to mercy in a year. In the fourth book, *Goblet of Fire,* Harry is initially consumed by thoughts of what others think of him—his external person. By book's end, after trials with his best friend, the Hogwarts student body, and a dragon, he is able to shrug off a front-page hatchet job in the wizarding world's main newspaper.

In *Order of the Phoenix,* Harry is consumed by a desire for news. He struggles to listen to the television, agonizes over the lack of reports from friends, and wanders his neighborhood in search of newspapers in trash cans. At the end, he is aware of his need to turn inward and to discover and strengthen his inner life. He knows that his dependence on the outer world was his point of vulnerability, which Voldemort used to manipulate him, and the weakness that helped cause his godfather's death.

Finally, when Harry comes onto the scene in *Half-Blood Prince,* he is half asleep as he waits for Dumbledore to come for him. At this point he is very much in doubt about Dumbledore's arrival and even about Dumbledore's care for him. At book's end, Harry is vigilant and braced to take on the mission Dumbledore has given him, and he confesses to the Minister of Magic Dumbledore's presence with him, even though the headmaster is dead. (For more on Dumbledore as a symbol of Christ, see "But Obviously Dumbledore Is Not Jesus" at www.Hogwarts Professor.com.)

Fourth, the design. Let me give you two quick examples of how the organization of the books parallels the alchemical work. First, let's compare the roles of sulfur and mercury in alchemy with the roles of Harry's friends Ron and Hermione in the books.

The alchemical work purifies a base metal by dissolving and recongealing the metal using two principal reagents, or catalysts. These reagents reflect the masculine and feminine polarities of existence. Alchemical sulfur represents the masculine, impulsive, and red pole, while alchemical mercury, or quicksilver, represents the feminine and cool complement. Together and separately these reagents advance the base metal to gold.

Harry's two closest friends are Ron Weasley, the redheaded, passionate boy, and Hermione Granger, the brilliant, cool young woman. They are also living symbols of alchemical sulfur (Ron) and mercury (Hermione's initials are "HG," the chemical sign for mercury, and her parents are both dentists, making the Hermes-Mercury connection complete!). Together, and more obviously in their disagreements and separation, Harry's friendships with Ron and Hermione transform him from lead to gold. Sulfur and quicksilver are frequently called "the quarreling couple," an apt name for Ron and Hermione.

The second example is the way the three stages of alchemy are illustrated in the cycle of each book. What has often been described as Harry's annual hero journey is actually the cycle of the alchemical transformation—and each stage of the work, in case you need a road sign, has a character named for it in the Harry Potter books. The first stage of the alchemical work is dissolution, usually called the *nigredo*, or black stage. In this black stage, "the body of the impure metal, the matter for the Stone, or the old, outmoded state of being is killed, putrefied, and dissolved into the original substance of creation, the *prima materia*, in order that it may be renovated and reborn in a new form."[3] Harry's godfather, Sirius Black, is named for this stage of the work.

The second stage is purification, usually called the *albedo*, or white work. It follows the ablution, or washing, of the prima materia, which causes it to turn a brilliant white. "When the matter reaches the albedo, it has become pure and spotless."[4] Albus Dumbledore (*albus* is Latin for "white, resplendent") is named for this stage of the work. Frequently used symbols of the albedo stage of the work include the moon or a lily. *Luna*, the Latin word for moon, is the name of one of Harry's friends in the fifth book, and *Lily* is the name of his mother, who gave her life to save his.

The third and last stage of the alchemical work is the recongealing or perfection, usually called the *rubedo*, or red stage.

The purified matter is now ready to be reunited with the spirit (or the already united spirit and soul). With the fixation, crystallization or embodiment of the eternal spirit, form is bestowed upon the pure, but as yet formless, matter of the Stone. At this union, the supreme chemical wedding, the body is resurrected into eternal life. As the heat of the fire is increased, the divine red tincture flushes the white Stone with its rich, red colour. . . . The reddening of the white matter is also frequently likened to staining with blood.[5]

Rubeus Hagrid (*rubeus* is Latin for "red") is named for this stage. A common symbol of the red work and the philosopher's stone is the red lion.

Each book thus far is a trip through these three stages. The black work, or dissolution, is the work done in Harry at Privet

Drive by the Dursleys and in the Hogwarts classroom by Snape, the teacher who seems to hate him. The white work, or purification, occurs under the watchful eye of the white alchemist Albus Dumbledore during Harry's year at Hogwarts. This often occurs in combination with painful separation from Ron, Hermione, or both. The red work, or rubedo, is the climactic crucible scene, so far always underground or in a graveyard, in which Harry dies a figurative death and is saved by love in the presence of a Christological symbol.

The resurrection at story's end each year is the culmination of that year's cycle and transformation. The cycle then closes with congratulations and explanations from the master alchemist and a return to the Dursleys for another trip through the cycle.

And fifth and last, the curious images throughout the books. Each of the wonderfully engaging events of the Triwizard Tournament and Harry's preparation for each trial by fire, water, or labyrinth in *Goblet of Fire* is from the alchemical work. A quick review of the tasks and search of guides to alchemical imagery in literature reveals the role of dragons, the egg, the prefects' bath and water trial, the labyrinth, and the graveyard resurrection and fight.[6]

> **Dragons:** The first task in the tournament involves dragons, which are used in alchemy to represent "matter at the *beginning* of the work being resolved into philosophical sulphur and mercury" (emphasis added).

> **The egg:** Harry and the other champions then have to solve the mystery of the egg, which appropriately is the name given to "the alchemist's vessel of transmutation in which the birth of the philosopher's stone takes place . . . also known as the griffin's egg" (i.e., from beginning to the place of the work).

The bath: Harry solves his egg puzzle in the prefects' bath/swimming pool, a word used by alchemists to describe "the secret, inner, invisible fire which dissolves and kills, cleanses and resurrects the matter of the Stone in the vessel" (what makes the work proceed in the alchemist's test tube).

Water immersion/flood: The second task in the tournament is the trial underwater in the lake. Interestingly, one of the alchemist's maxims was "Perform no operation until all be made water."[7] Water immersion, it turns out, is "a symbol of the dissolution and putrefaction of the matter of the Stone during the black nigredo stage" (we're seeing some progress from preparatory dragons to the action of the first stage).

Labyrinth: The third task, which is supposed to be the end of the tournament, is a maze and is a metaphor for life in the world, or "the dangerous journey of the alchemist through the opus alchymicum. . . . While in the labyrinth of the opus, illusion and confusion reign and the alchemist is in danger of losing all connection and clarity" (we end with an image of the whole work).

Grave: Harry and Cedric are transported to the graveyard, where they witness Voldemort's rebirthing party. The graveyard is also what alchemists and poets refer to as "the alchemist's vessel during the nigredo," when everything is broken down into formless elements—a fine metaphor for what happens to Harry there.[8]

All the alchemical images of Harry's Triwizard tasks are preparatory for and descriptions of the black stage of the Great Work, or nigredo, to come in *Order of the Phoenix*. For more alchemical imagery, see the discussions of each book in chapters 12–17.

CONCLUSION: ALCHEMY AND THE POPULARITY OF HARRY POTTER

The following chart summarizes what we've learned about alchemy and Rowling's use of alchemical imagery in the Harry Potter novels.

The reason good authors use these alchemical images isn't from acute cleverness or chronic arcane-o-philia; it's because the three stages of the alchemical process and the whole "Great Work" of

ALCHEMY AND THE POPULARITY OF HARRY POTTER

ALCHEMY	Stage 1	Stage 2	Stage 3
PROCESS	Dissolution of lead or base metal	Action of contraries, Purification process	Gold, Philosopher's Stone, Red Lion
COLOR (STAGES)	Black (Nigredo)	White (Albedo)	Red (Rubedo)
ACTION	Dissolution	Purification	Perfection
IN HARRY POTTER			
CHARACTERS	Dursleys, Snape, House of Black	Albus Dumbledore, Remus Lupin	Rubeus Hagrid
HARRY'S SCENES	Privet Drive, Potions class, Umbridge	Solving mystery at Hogwarts	Crucible scenes, denouement
CHRISTIAN PARALLELS	Repentance	Baptism	Sanctification
CHRISTIAN VIRTUES	Humility, Obedience, Renunciation	Illumination, Purification, Moral Virtue	Theosis

alchemy parallels the spiritual work necessary for human beings in this life. As you can see in the chart above, the black stage represents repentance, humility, obedience, and renunciation. The white work is illumination and purification. The red work, rarely realized in this life but part of the human design nonetheless, is sanctity in God's glory through his graces.

Great writers in the English tradition use alchemical imagery because it helps them connect with that place in our heart designed to respond to the Great Story and promise of our life in Christ. This is so much a part of us that, though we are largely immunized to this message by our culture and schooling, we respond with joy and longing to the imaginative shadows of it in fiction. This is why, perhaps more than any other books of our time, the Harry Potter series baptizes the imagination, touches our heart, and fosters this longing within us. Far from preparing a generation of candidates for New Age apostasy, these books have baptized the imagination of hundreds of millions and nourished the faith of readers who believe.

5

ONE PERSON, TWO NATURES

*Doppelgängers point to the struggle of
dual natures—and their resolution in the God-Man.*

I enjoy speaking with Rowling's readers, young and old, for a variety of reasons. To be honest, a great many in every audience I speak to—from schools and bookstores to churches and fan conventions—know the books much better than I do, so I always learn something. Then there's the fun of talking about a great story and its meaning (either to me personally or in the grand scheme of things) with thoughtful people; really, I live for those times.

What they tell me they get out of the talks, besides the kick they get out of reminding me again how to pronounce Hermione's name (you'd think I was Viktor Krum), is seeing the stories diagonally. By that I mean seeing the common elements of all the books rather than thinking of the stories in narrative sequences of event after event. Certainly the hero's journey and alchemical formula is a "wow" to them, but the biggest wow comes when we begin to talk about *doppelgängers*.

"Doppel-whatzits?" I feel a little bit like Hagrid with one of his nasty pets when I introduce that word. Anyway, it just means "double-go-er" in German, and there really isn't an English equivalent. The term is used to describe a "shadow character." A doppelgänger is a creature's complementary figure or shadow, which reveals aspects of its character otherwise invisible. Think of Robert Louis Stevenson's Dr. Jekyll and Mr. Hyde and Mary W. Shelley's Dr. Frankenstein and his monster. Rowling has created doppelgängers that, like Jekyll/Hyde, are in the same body, and at least one, like Frankenstein and monster, that is in separate bodies.

You might find one, maybe two, shadow characters in a common novel, but almost every character in Harry Potter is something of a doppelgänger. Specifically, the Harry/Voldemort relation is key to understanding the meaning of the books and why they are so popular. Let's take a look first at how pervasive this idea really is in the books' characters and then take a close look at Harry and his dark shadow.

Many of Rowling's characters, for instance, are *animagi.* These are masters of the magical subject of Transfiguration who can change at will into an animal shape. The animagi we know of include James Potter (white stag), Sirius Black (black dog), Peter Pettigrew (rat), Minerva McGonagall (cat), Rita Skeeter (bug). We know Albus Dumbledore was a Transfiguration Master, as well as being an accomplished alchemist. However, in *Half-Blood Prince,* he died without revealing if he was a white bumblebee animagus (his name means "white bumblebee") or the tawny owl that appears in several places throughout the series. Perhaps his portrait will tell us in the last book!

This shape-changing stunt is not just a plot device or part of every magical novel's repertoire. The shape each animagus takes is a pointer to its character; for example, Peter Pettigrew, who is a rat animagus, is the rat fink who betrayed the Potters to Voldemort. The animal figure is a shadow, or doppelgänger, that allows us to see more clearly the outline of the true person. Rowling, via this second figure or shape of the person, gives us a clearer look at what may not be so obvious from the first view.

A variant on animagi is the Patronus shape each character projects. The Patronus Charm, *"Expecto Patronum!"* produces an animal figure and is the only effective defense against the soul-sucking dementors. Harry's Patronus quite appropriately is a white stag.[1] Cho Chang's is a swan, and Hermione's is an otter.[2]

Doppelgängers of the Jekyll and Hyde sort (meaning the shadow is an aspect within a person rather than another person) are often a simple matter of birth. Harry's world is populated with what Delores Umbridge hates: "half-breeds." Rubeus Hagrid and Olympe Maxime, for instance, are the children of giants and magical persons ("half giants"). Fleur Delacour's grandmother was a Veela (a beautiful woman who grows a beak and scaly wings when enraged). Then there are witches and wizards born from Muggle parents; Lily Evans Potter and Hermione Granger are the most notable Muggle-born characters, and Colin Creevy and his brother have to be the most fun.

Tom Riddle, aka Lord Voldemort, is a half-breed as well, because his mother was a witch and his father a Muggle. (That his own followers are unaware of this suggests he has concealed his double life.) Harry has an honorary membership to this club because, though both his parents were magical persons, his mom was Muggle-born, he grew up with Muggles, and for many years he was totally unaware of his magical heritage or abilities.

In addition to these half-breeds and shape-changers, we also have a category of shape-changers that do so because of their birthright or because of some tragic occurrence. Nymphadora Tonks is a *metamorphmagus* who is able to change shape at will, which is a handy trick for disguise in her work as an Auror. Remus Lupin, much less fortunately, is a werewolf who is only able to control his dangerous transformations by way of difficult and ill-tasting potions. Rowling has left clues in every book, some quite open, that suggest Severus Snape is a half vampire (though she has insisted in interviews that he is not a full-blooded vampire à la Count Sanguini). If this is not a MacGuffin or a red herring, then the "Half-Blood Prince," aka Severus Snape also has a meaningful shadow life, in addition to his being a double agent.

And there are more!

The books also include a host of "threshold characters" whom scholars call *liminal.* These folk stand in the doorway between two worlds, which amounts to their living in two worlds or so far to the periphery of their own world that they cannot fit into the usual categories (good guy or bad guy, insider or outsider, for instance). Severus Snape is a good example, half vampire or no. The Potions Master, as a former(?) Death Eater and member of the Order of the Phoenix, lives and moves in both supposedly exclusive domains. Other threshold doppelgängers include the other Death Eaters and Dumbledore supporters (all of whom conceal their loyalties), the Dursleys, Dobby, Winky, Firenze, Neville Longbottom, the Squibs (Argus Filch and Arabella Figg), Mundungus Fletcher, and Percy Weasley.

And of course there is Polyjuice Potion. By means of this magical draught, Harry Potter characters can for a brief time transform into other characters. Ron and Harry become Crabbe and Goyle in order to visit the Slytherin common room in *Chamber of Secrets,* and Barty Crouch Jr. hoodwinks all of Hogwarts into thinking he's Alastor "Mad-Eye" Moody for the whole of *Goblet of Fire.*

I think the only Jekyll/Hyde folk I haven't mentioned are those who aren't "folks." Rowling's menagerie of magical creatures includes a host of half-breed, double-natured creatures. The centaurs, with the head and chest of a man and the body and legs of a horse, are a notable example, as are the merpeople, hippogriffs, and the sphinx (who makes a cameo appearance in *Goblet of Fire*). Though not exactly half-breeds, special mention should be made of the phoenix, thestrals, and unicorns in the Potter books, because they are not what they seem—namely, bird or horse or even bird/horse/dragon.

Now for the pairs. So far all the shadow characters or doppelgängers I have mentioned have been internal ones; that is, the mirrored aspects are within a single person or creature. It is just as common for there to be two persons, in which the one is a revealing reflection of the other (again, Dr. Frankenstein and his monster are a good example of this shadowing).

In Harry Potter, Rowling sets up quite a few such pairs for our consideration. Besides the obvious sets of twins (Fred and George Weasley, the Patil sisters), other notable Potter pairs include:

- Slytherin and Gryffindor (opposing houses)
- Hagrid and Grawp (giant brothers)
- Draco and Dudley (frequently paired in Harry's mind)
- Harry and Draco (generational leaders of opposing houses)
- Sirius and James (Harry's godfather and father)
- Ron and Hermione (friends with opposing personalities)
- Hagrid and Harry (two orphans at Hogwarts)
- Lily and Petunia (opposing mother figures)
- Peter and Neville (a cross-generational pair of look-alikes)
- Harry and Neville (joined by the prophecy)

Rowling has paired these characters, be it through hatred or mutual delight, for a reason. While many authors use this writing device to highlight one conflict or draw the reader further into the drama, *Rowling uses it everywhere.* Look at the list above; have we left anybody out? The only people not animagi, half-breeds, characters living in the borderlands between communities, or pairs, are Nazis.

Not literally Nazis, of course. I mean witches and wizards, self-styled "purebloods" who hate Muggle-born magical persons and "half-breed" magical creatures. Dolores Umbridge personifies this spirit of eugenics in the magical community, in which the concern for purity of blood marks even families that don't openly support Voldemort and the Death Eaters.

So what? I suppose the case could be made that everything in existence evidences some sort of polarity (male/female, tall/short, etc.). Maybe you can even screw yourself up into a knot and believe that *all* these pairings and doppelgänger figures in the Potter novels (and the central conflict between purebreds and half-breeds) are a remarkable coincidence.

Except that the outcomes of the books hinge on the relation of Harry and Voldemort, a classic doppelgänger pairing. Understanding this specific pairing helps us to understand why the rest of the book is crammed with half-breeds, outsiders, and orphans. The Harry/Voldemort shadow, the pivotal antagonism of the series, points to the duality in every human being and the answer to this fallen state in the God-man, Jesus Christ.

THE HARRY/VOLDEMORT DOPPELGÄNGER

Order of the Phoenix begins with three mentions of Harry's feeling that his skull has been split in two, and one has to imagine it must crack right down that jagged scar on his forehead. It turns out, as we learn by book's end, that Harry's head really is divided and he has an unwelcome guest. He isn't carrying a passenger like Quirrell, nor is he possessed as was Ginny in *Chamber of Secrets.* Rather, Harry has a double nature, or shadow, in his link to Voldemort—and his inability to turn inward and confront this shadow is the cause of the tragedy in *Order of the Phoenix*'s battle royal.

Harry's literal schizophrenia or double-mindedness with Voldemort really evidences itself in *Order of the Phoenix*, but each of the preceding books hints at it. Harry's scar—the mark he received from the curse that failed to kill him as an infant—always burns, for instance, when Voldemort is in a rage. Harry has the ability (known as *Parseltongue*) to speak to snakes from Voldemort via the curse. And quite a few times Harry has been able to see the goings-on in Lord Voldemort's surroundings in his dreams (as in the opening to *Goblet of Fire*). *Order of the Phoenix* just marks the first times that the Dark Lord took advantage of his tie with Harry to manipulate his thinking.

We also learn in *Order of the Phoenix* that Harry and Voldemort were initially joined by a prophecy. It had been foretold just before Harry's birth that "the one with the power to vanquish the Dark Lord approaches" and that either the Dark Lord or his prophesied vanquisher "must die at the hands of the other."[3] Harry, it seems, must kill his ugly relation or be killed. Because Rowling has guaranteed that there will only be seven Harry Potter novels, a lot of fans are concerned that Harry's future looks dim.

As I argued in chapter 2, Harry and Voldemort, besides being doppelgängers, are both representatives of the primeval Gryffindor/Slytherin feud. Though it isn't certain, Rowling has left clues in each book that Harry is also the Heir of Gryffindor. We learn in *Chamber of Secrets* that Voldemort is certainly the Heir of Slytherin. Voldemort has a split history, but his blue blood comes through his magical mom (who died at his birth).

We will interpret names further in chapter 10, but it will help here to recall that Voldemort is not the Dark Lord's given name. His real name is Tom Riddle, which, because *Thomas* comes from the Aramaic word for "twin," is a pointer to how important the doppelgänger structure is to these stories. Voldemort's given name means "twin enigma."

The *riddle* we have to solve, then, is what meaning, if any, is there to this doubling or *twin* motif in Harry Potter? A fascinating meaning, really, and one that is quite explicitly Christian.

Alchemy helps unwrap the riddle. As you'll recall, the principal activity of alchemy is the chemical marriage of the imbalanced "arguing couple": masculine sulfur and feminine quicksilver. These two qualities have to be reconciled and resolved ("die" and be "reborn") before they can be rejoined in a perfected golden unity. Opposites have to be reconciled and resolved for there to be a new life. *One part of a pairing or both must die for there to be new life.* Alchemists frequently cited Christ's words: "Verily, verily, I say unto you, except a corn of wheat fall into the ground and die, it abideth alone: but if it die, it bringeth forth much fruit" (John 12:24, KJV). Alchemists took this verse and the hope of eternal life in Christ's death and resurrection as scriptural confirmation that their doctrines were correct.

The answer to the twin riddle (and the reason we swim in shadow figures in these books) is that Harry and Voldemort are opposites, and specifically they are Saint Paul's "old self" and "new self" (Ephesians 4:22-24). Just as the old man must decrease or die in us that Christ may become greater and live in our heart, so one or both of the Harry/Voldemort pair must be slain (Voldemort alone, I hope!) if the other is to live.

Rowling makes this all but explicit in chapter 21 of *Order of the Phoenix*. Harry has just witnessed while dreaming (through his mind link with Voldemort) the snake attack on Arthur Weasley. He tells the tale to Dumbledore and, while waiting for magical transit to Grimmauld Place, watches the headmaster do a smoke augury.

The smoke auguror puffs out some smoke, which takes the shape of a serpent's head, mouth wide open. Dumbledore murmurs, "Naturally, naturally" and asks, "But in essence divided?" The smoke serpent answers in the affirmative by neatly splitting into two snakes.

Interpreting the smoke snake augury is pretty straightforward. Dumbledore's first question to the auguror was about Harry's assertion that "I was the snake. . . . I saw it all from the snake's point of view." The question Dumbledore asks the auguror was, perhaps, "Is there a shared nature here between Voldemort and this young man?" The single smoke-serpent form suggests the answer from the auguror is, "Yes, there is! They share a serpent nature."

"But in essence divided?" Again, a "yes" answer. *One nature, two essences.*

Perhaps that phrase doesn't make you sit up and slap your forehead. Folks don't kill each other anymore (or as often, at least) over who Jesus is, so I guess that's understandable. But when they did, the fight was often about the nature and essence of the Christ.

The first great heresy in Christianity was the Arian heresy, in which a priest named Arius argued that Christ was not God in essence and that he had only a human nature. The heretics tended to square off by reducing Christ to *either* a divine nature but not really human *or* a human nature but not really divine. The church insisted (Council of Chalcedon, AD 451) that Christ has two natures, *both* fully divine *and* fully human. In his divine nature, he was able to conquer sin and death and rise again; in his human nature, we are able to share in his resurrection and inherit eternal life: *one divine essence, two perfect natures.*

Back to Harry and his bad twin, Tom. When Dumbledore gets the message from the auguror that Harry and Voldemort are one in nature and two in essence, what are we to make of that?

First, we can see that Harry and Voldemort are a doppelgänger pair according to the "new self in Christ/old self in sin" model. They have the same nature certainly—the *fallen* nature we all have as a result of the sin in the Garden. Second, we can see that Harry is moving toward resolution of this struggle of two natures by choosing life, not death; Tom Riddle has chosen the way of death—an essential difference.

This difference is only made clearer by the revelations of Lord Voldemort's pursuit of immortality via the creation of six Horcruxes, in which he inserts a piece of his soul into an object after murdering another human being. This path of death has made Lord Thingy into something hardly human. Harry's choice of life and what is good, in contrast, has made him even more clearly an image of his "father in heaven" and what Dumbledore calls "pure in heart" (compare to Matthew 5:8) and "a soul that is untarnished and whole."[4]

Another way to describe the answer to the "one nature, two essences" problem is with a simple alchemical solution. You do it every morning when you get in the shower. Really. You turn on the hot water, and when it gets warm, you jump in. Then, of course, the hot water really kicks in and you're being cooked— so you turn on the cold water (just enough so you can enjoy the shower). You find a balance of hot and cold water by pairing the opposites. Too hot? Add cold. Too cold? Add hot. The opposite quality is the answer. Think like Goldilocks.

What is the answer to Harry's double-mindedness, that is, his being one in nature but two in essence with Voldemort? Just like the shower, the answer is the opposite. The solution to the twin riddle of "one in nature, two in essence" is the God-man—he who is "two in nature and one in essence." This is the solution for *all* the double-natured folk in Rowling's creation and for the characters who deny their own duality (the purebloods)—and for us, the readers, who also struggle with conflicting natures.

Almost every character in the Potter books is a doppelgänger of one sort or another. The key conflict of the books is Harry's prophesied pairing with Voldemort. Dumbledore spells out for us that Harry and his "old man" are a single image of what all fallen human beings are—double-minded creatures in which the new man and old man struggle for mastery.

The Harry Potter books are loaded with alchemy and doppelgänger characters, which for Christians provide imaginative pictures of our fallen human condition and point to the redemptive solution in Christ. Readers young and old relate and respond to these pictures because, consciously or unconsciously, they recognize themselves in these characters. The stories connect with what Blaise Pascal called the God-shaped vacuum in human hearts.

Dumbledore points to Christ—as the solution of the existential problem all human beings share with Harry and friends—in the language Dumbledore uses to describe the problem; the themes and symbolism of the books, as the next few chapters will demonstrate, take us to that key to which Dumbledore points and for which our heart is designed.

6

CHRISTIAN ANSWERS
TO BIG QUESTIONS

*Surprise endings suggest a remedy
for the evils of prejudice.*

Looking for God in Harry Potter is not *The English Major's Guide to Harry Potter* (which, yes, I am writing). This book lacks, consequently, discussions of narratological perspective, three-dimensional theme work, and the all-important influence of previous writers. By choosing to focus on the Christian content of English literature, in which context the Harry Potter books have been written, I have had to leave out a lot of stuff.

Which is, of course, as it should be. (Buy a book on polar bears, you don't want to find out it's really a treatise on the geometry in Gothic cathedrals.) I do, however, need to discuss the principal themes of the books. Their Christian meaning is relatively self-evident; the trouble is keeping people in the room when you use the word *themes.*

Briefly, here's how I decide if a book is a "classic" or not. My "Great Book" test has three parts:

- Does it address the big questions of human life?
- Does the artistry of the work support the answers given to these questions?
- Are the answers correct? (This last, in light of historic English literature, can be rephrased, "Are the answers Christian?")

The Harry Potter books are classics—and not just as "kid-lit" but as classics of world literature. The tales are masterfully told, at least in terms of how carefully the books and series have been structured, and they carry a mother lode of meaning. Which brings us to what English teachers call themes.

Themes are just the questions authors try to answer in story form. The larger the question and the more important it is for us to understand the answer is a decent gauge of whether the book is worth reading. We know the Potter books have been ingeniously plotted and are engaging enough to have sold more than 300 million copies; the subject for discussion, then, is what is in these beautiful, best-selling wheelbarrows?

In them, we find the answer to four principal questions:

- How are we to treat one another?
- What is the answer to the mystery of death?
- When are we to embrace change or flee change?
- What makes a human being good or bad, or even human?

Teachers give these questions "theme" titles like Pride and Prejudice, Death and Bereavement, Personal Transformation, and Choice. And these are the four overarching themes in the Harry Potter novels. In the next three chapters, I will look briefly at each before discussing the Christian meaning of Rowling's answer.

Rowling has special sympathy for the victims of prejudice and ill treatment. Her favorite writers are Jane Austen and Charles Dickens, who champion the downtrodden and underdogs in every one of their books. Before her writing career took off, Rowling worked professionally on behalf of the helpless at Amnesty International, the worldwide advocacy arm and voice of political prisoners and the unjustly persecuted and tortured everywhere. Closer to home, Rowling experienced the agony of losing friends who avoided her during the degenerative illness of her mother. She also endured the public shaming of single mothers during the Margaret Thatcher/ John Major years. Since her success, her largest public gifts have been to causes supporting single mothers and those with AIDS. Her heart and her money go to underdogs on the periphery of society. No surprise, then, to find out that prejudice—its cause, effect, and cure—is a primary focus in the Harry Potter novels.

As is evident in the chart on page 56, every one of the Harry Potter books reveals a prejudice against another downtrodden group of people who are different from "normal" wizards or Muggles in big ways and small.

Rowling doesn't just lay out a black-and-white world where the good guys aren't racist and the bad guys are. Only Dumbledore seems free of prejudice. Hagrid doesn't trust foreigners or Muggles, though he is hated because he is a half giant. Ron, despite his insecurities about being poor, has a host of wizarding prejudices from giants to werewolves (though he only knows—and likes—one of each) and is always the first to point his finger at someone he doesn't like. Harry's "age-old prejudice," as Lupin puts it, against Severus Snape and Draco Malfoy is his heroic flaw, and it is the only prejudice explored in *Half-Blood Prince* that prepares us for Harry's struggle in the final chapter.

And the prisoners of prejudice, mostly the Slytherins, seem so

PREJUDICE IN HARRY POTTER

Book	Prejudice Against	Origin	Object
Sorcerer's Stone	Abnormal or magical folk	Dursleys	Harry & Hagrid
	Non-magical folk (Muggles)	Slytherins	Muggles
	Poor	Malfoys	Weasleys
	Clumsy, awkward, stupid	Draco	Neville
Chamber of Secrets	Mudbloods (Muggle parent)	Slytherins	Hermione & others
	Squibs (magic-born Muggle)	Magic folk	Argus Filch
	Ugly, unpopular	Olive Hornby	Moaning Myrtle
	The Nearly Headless	Headless ghosts	Nick
Prisoner of Azkaban	Prisoners	Everyone	Sirius Black
	Werewolves	Almost everyone	Remus Lupin
	Hippogriffs	Ministry of Magic	Buckbeak
	Intelligent women	Boys & Teachers	Hermione
Goblet of Fire	Young people	Fleur	Harry
	Giants	Magic folk	Hagrid & Maxime
	Foreigners	Hagrid	Triwizard guests
	Unprejudiced	Death Eaters	Albus & Weasleys
Order of the Phoenix	Harry supporters	Ministry of Magic	Order & Harry's friends
	Alternative press	*Daily Prophet*	Quibbler & Luna
	Centaurs and half-breeds	Umbridge	Firenze
	Giants	Everyone	Grawp
	Nonconformists	Teaching establishment	Fred/George & Trelawney
Half-Blood Prince	Severus Snape	James Potter/Sirius Black/Harry Potter	Severus Snape

unhappy in their sarcasm and meanness that they are more to be pitied than despised.

What is remarkable about the magical world of Harry Potter, then, is not so much the incredible creatures, structures, and enchantments as it is the fact that the wizards and witches are as unloving and self-important as the Muggles many of them despise (and all patronize). Good thing the magic folk have an enlightened government and a free press to stand up for the oppressed!

Ha! Pardon my sarcasm. The *Daily Prophet* is the television news and newspaper media conglomerate for wizards and witches. Every book chronicles the way it spreads half-truths and misinformation as gospel wisdom "hot off the press." In *Goblet of Fire*, though, we learn that these are not just the inevitable mistakes from rushing news to print. Meeting Rita Skeeter, star reporter for the *Prophet* and other wizarding publications (*Witch Weekly*, for one), we realize that errors that might have been caused by incompetence or negligence are the result of plain and simple wickedness.

Take a look at Rita's name for a clue as to what she's about: *Rita* = "read-a," *Skeeter* = "squito, mosquito, or bloodsucking-disease-carrying-parasitical bug." And Rita is equal to her name. Rather than exposing the unjust and prejudiced in defense of the downtrodden, Ms. Skeeter, an illegal "beetle bug" animagus, does everything she can to make life miserable for those in positions of responsibility or who are somehow different. She loves to create hardship for the Ministry, of course, but saves her special venom for individuals she dislikes. In *Goblet of Fire* she writes unflattering, unkind, and rude pieces, several of which she makes up whole cloth, about Dumbledore, Hagrid, Hermione, and Harry, who is misrepresented once and crucified another time on the morning of the last Triwizard task.

Thus the media in the magical world (I think we are meant to ask, "Unlike our own?") is not about the life-supporting mission of exposing prejudice and uplifting those beaten down by it. As we learn in *Order of the Phoenix*, the newspaper instead actively and intentionally creates or fosters prejudice against individuals and groups in toadying service to the government. Cornelius Fudge wants Harry and Dumbledore discredited? The *Daily Prophet* is there to package the news daily for weeks on end—and on a different cue from the Ministry, tells a story saying the complete opposite without a blush for the lies and distortions of the previous months.

The reading public acts on cue from the shadow casters and

either attacks or passively agrees to thinking less of the misrepresented. Remember how Hermione is treated by Mrs. Weasley after the *Witch Weekly* article portrayed her as a scarlet woman? And Harry's reception at Hogwarts in *Order of the Phoenix* after a summer of innuendo that he is a braggart and show-off in need of attention? Even the good and wise have their opinions made-to-order and prejudices confirmed by the popular media. Only media-savvy Hermione figures out how to manipulate the system by having Harry's interview printed in the alternative press. The media in Harry Potter's world is key in attacking the downtrodden and furthering prejudice (just as it often is in our own world).

The Ministry of Magic (MOM), one assumes from its initials, is supposed to be the protector of the helpless and a force for good against evil in the world. However, the Ministry (I think we are again meant to ask, "Unlike our own government?") is anything but maternal or heroic. Rowling consistently represents them as a gaggle of self-important airheads busying themselves with laughable trivia (cauldron bottom reports) or international bread-and-circus functions like the Quidditch World Cup, while neglecting to take care of even their own. Just how long was Bertha Jorkins missing before the Ministry sent out a search party?

But the Ministry is worse than bumbling and distracted. In *Chamber of Secrets,* in response to pressure and the need to appear active, Minister of Magic Cornelius Fudge has Hagrid imprisoned in Azkaban, though he knows Hagrid is innocent. In *Goblet of Fire,* Sirius Black reveals that his life sentence in Azkaban was handed down just for the appearance of acting with strength. Stan Shunpike's imprisonment under the new law-and-order regime of Rufus Scrimgeour in *Half-Blood Prince* shows us the Ministry has learned nothing about how to resist evil effectively. Azkaban is a psychic concentration camp where few survive. The Ministry, it turns out, had been torturing those imprisoned in Azkaban through the guards, the dementors, who lived by sucking everything good and beautiful from their souls. These guards return to Lord Voldemort's service on his return and are rapidly reproducing, as we learn in *Half-Blood Prince,* causing all of Britain to fall into a joyless depression. The name of the prison itself is a magical turn on Alcatraz and gulag-rich Soviet republics such as Uzbekistan.

The Ministry has its comic front, then, but a gulag back. Ambitious ministers fiddle with inconsequential matters and act in response to pressure generated by the rich and the media. The Ministry is incapable of passing the Muggle Protection Act or of policing wizards practicing dark magic and Muggle baiting. Those who press for this sort of "social good" legislation are demoted for lacking "real wizard pride." And beyond its failure to protect the innocent, in its nightmarish prison and zeal to incarcerate the innocent, the Ministry becomes the agent of discrimination and persecution of the defenseless. The modern, Orwellian regime with MOM's face!

It is a great disappointment but little surprise when the Minister of Magic, in the dark hour at the end of *Goblet of Fire*—a time requiring decisiveness and courage to combat the risen Lord Voldemort—shows himself an impotent coward and fool. In a world (unlike our own?) ruled by prejudices and stereotypes, a world whose thoughts and feelings are guided by a self-serving media, and a world whose government maintains order by fear of tortuous imprisonment, don't look for public figures of the stature of Winston Churchill. *Order of the Phoenix* is a dark novel, not because the bad guys are so bad—they are largely invisible—but because the supposed good guys have black hearts, which makes the life of the truly virtuous a catacomb nightmare. Though Fudge acknowledges in the *Daily Prophet* at the end of *Order of the Phoenix* that the Dark Lord is back and the magical world is ready to oppose him, little has changed. The new Minister of

Magic, Rufus Scrimgeour, whom we meet in *Half-Blood Prince*, is a get-tough politician who resembles Churchill in appearance but who rearranges deck chairs while Albus Dumbledore is effectively researching and resisting Lord Voldemort.

These are kids' books? Hardly. The message of Harry Potter is clear: Poisonous prejudice is everywhere, and only constant vigilance and resistance to the regime of ideas (whose government and media authorities foster and codify this hatred) will free us of it. The Harry Potter books encourage readers to take a step back from the world and recognize what an unloving place it is. This stepping back to appreciate the satirical picture of our world drawn in story is the first step necessary to a posture essential to the Christian walk, namely, being "in the world" but not "of the world" (John 17:13-16).

Look again at the chart listing the prejudices of the wizarding world and the persecuted individuals and groups who live there. Only in *Order of the Phoenix* do we learn (in the House of Black, looking at the Black family tapestry) how inbred and insular the leading magical families have become over the generations and how far their narrow belief in eugenics, or "good breeding," to overcome the world's ills had taken them—that is, into the Dark Lord's service. We can see this same thinking reflected in modern society. It is responsible for the Soviet gulags, Nazi camps, and abortion clinics, and it's this same thinking that continues to drive our culture of death (euthanasia, abortion, self-sterilization, etc.).

But why do we get so much out of hearing such a difficult message? Adult and child readers who rarely read such long novels are reading these novels repeatedly, and I mean again and again and again. There has to be a reason such a painful message about our times is much more than reader-friendly. I think there are two reasons.

First, the hook. Nothing is worse than being preached at in a novel (okay, there are a lot of things worse than that, but among reading headaches, a writer on a philosophical or theological hobby-horse is way up there). Rowling lulls one almost to sleep with all the persecuted groups and individuals and how wicked she makes the bad guys. Yawn! The good guys are the victims of prejudice, the bad guys are all proud and prejudiced, what's to keep one awake?

The revelation to come is that we are the prejudiced ones. Every Potter novel ends with an Agatha Christie surprise. These surprise endings make the dullest reader slap himself in the forehead and say, "Duh! What was I thinking? I should have known that bad guy was a good guy! Why was I so sure he was a bad apple?"

This gives Rowling's prejudice theme a third dimension: the dimension above the page and in your heart. It's one thing to hate Draco along with Harry and his gang because of his Nazi-like snobbery—it's another thing entirely to learn that you're as bad as Draco for having assumed that the bad guy was good and the good guy was bad (which Rowling tricks us into doing in almost every book, and especially in *Half-Blood Prince*, in which we are tricked into believing Severus Snape is a murderer and Horace Slughorn is on the side of the angels).[1]

The second reason we respond to the agonizing problem of prejudice in the world is more to the point. We read and reread the books because they offer the right answer. That answer is love. Prejudice or a rush to judgment is a failure in love. We recognize in these stories the desire to see what makes us feel best about ourselves even if it means being unkind or dismissive of others. The Sorting Hat, Hermione, and Dumbledore all make pleas in *Order of the Phoenix* for students to overlook their differences for the greater good—pleas for love which mostly fall on deaf ears. Though it has prevented him from being the Dumbledore man he imagines himself to be, Harry's hatred for Severus Snape—his prejudice—is what largely defines him at the end of *Half-Blood Prince*. If Rowling is true to her theme,

Harry's ability to defeat the Dark Lord will largely depend on his having overcome the darkness within himself.

Love is the defining mark of Christians: "By this shall all men know that ye are my disciples" (John 13:35, KJV). One of the few explicit commandments given by Christ to his followers is the love of God and neighbor (Mark 12:30-31). Another commandment, really an application of the commandment to love, is the prohibition against judging our brother's sins (Matthew 7:1-5). This is not a prohibition of discernment and virtuous discrimination, but the warning against identifying our neighbor by his sins and the pretense of being without sin ourselves.

Just as Christ is the answer to the "twin riddle," so he is also the answer to the prejudice nightmare. Christ is Love himself, and as much as he lives in our heart, like him we stand with the underdogs of society, resist the Pharisees and forces of this world, and are called to love others as ourselves, that is, unconditionally and sacrificially. Christ never conforms to the prejudices of his times or shrinks to being a respecter of persons or position. His disciples are called to a no less heroic position—and the Harry Potter books, in their satire of worldly institutions and exposure of our own rush to judge and condemn, point to this life in Christ.

But being against prejudice and for love is a little bit like being against drunk driving. Christians are against drunk driving, but so are sentimental nihilists and Christian-baiting communists. In the theme and treatment of death, and in the means to transcend death, the Potter books move from implicit support of the Christian understanding of the world to almost explicit statements of doctrine.

7

THE TRIUMPH OF
LOVE OVER DEATH

The mystery of death meets the ultimate answer.

The Halloween murders of James and Lily Potter can be taken as the starting point of the Harry Potter stories, and death has never been far from the reader's line of sight. As we've already discussed, Harry dies a figurative death in each book. *Goblet of Fire, Order of the Phoenix,* and *Half-Blood Prince* feature the violent deaths of characters readers have come to love, and when we leave Harry at the end of the last two books, he is struggling with the meaning of death. Which is what all Harry Potter readers should be doing.

Harry Potter is about love and death, but if I had to choose one over the other, I'd say the books are about death. Why am I so sure? Well, on this subject, Rowling has been very open. She has said, "In fact, death and bereavement and what death means, I would say, is one of the central themes in all seven books."[1] Can't be much plainer than that. Why would a young woman in the bloom of life write a series of books about death and bereavement?

The best guess I've read is the commonsense one: she has experienced the death of loved ones and has something to say.

Every book develops the theme of love trumping death. Let's stroll through the books with Harry and see how he is learning that love is the power that defeats death—and how the Dark Lord is missing this lesson.

DEATH IN *HARRY POTTER AND THE SORCERER'S STONE*

Albus Dumbledore, the greatest wizard of the age and headmaster of Hogwarts, has two heart-to-heart talks with Harry during his first year at Hogwarts. The first is after Harry has discovered the Mirror of Erised, and the second is at book's end after Harry defeats Professor Quirrell in front of the Mirror. Dumbledore explains to Harry that he has destroyed the Stone. This shocks Harry because he knows that Dumbledore's friends, Nicolas Flamel and his wife, are only alive because of the Elixir of Life they get from the Stone. Dumbledore explains to Harry that "to the well organized mind, death is but the next great adventure."[2]

This definition of death—how to think of it rather than fear it—is the only part of this conversation repeated word for word in Harry's account to Ron and Hermione later. Harry then asks how it was possible for him to defeat Professor Quirrell, whose hands burned at the touch of Harry's skin. Dumbledore tells him it is love.

> *"Your mother died to save you. If there is one thing Voldemort cannot understand, it is love. He didn't realize that love as powerful as your mother's for you leaves its own mark. Not a scar, no visible sign . . . to have been loved so deeply, even though the person who loved us is gone, will give us some protection forever. It is in your very skin. Quirrell, full of*

hatred, greed and ambition, sharing his soul with Voldemort, could not touch you for this reason. It was agony to touch a person marked by something so good."[3]

In the opening book of the seven-book series, then, Rowling offers explicit teaching of what death is, and the importance of the love of those departed that continues to protect us even in their absence. Especially when this love was a *sacrificial* love.

DEATH IN *HARRY POTTER AND THE CHAMBER OF SECRETS*

Harry's meetings with Dumbledore in the next book include a short discussion in the headmaster's office and another after Harry fights the young Voldemort and his pet basilisk. Neither talk is about death. Harry does have a near-death scene, however, in *Chamber of Secrets*. He was wounded by the basilisk as he killed it and Voldemort/Riddle taunts him as he "dies."

As it turns out, Harry is saved by the healing tears of the phoenix Fawkes, Dumbledore's pet. Harry, facing certain death in combat with an older and wiser wizard, not to mention his giant, poisonous pet basilisk, triumphs through loyalty to Dumbledore and the graceful help of Fawkes. Believe it or not, this is an implicit, symbolic teaching on how to escape death through love, which I'll discuss at some length in chapter 12 on *Chamber of Secrets*.

DEATH IN *HARRY POTTER AND THE PRISONER OF AZKABAN*

The title of *Prisoner of Azkaban* is meaningful, but it might have been titled *Harry Potter and the Dementors* because so much of it turns on Harry's meeting with these soul-sucking monsters. The dementors raise in their victims their most painful memories in order to sap them of joy and hope; for Harry that memory is a reliving of his parents' murders. Harry fears this replayed experience more than he does Lord Voldemort; the pain of seeing his parents die again is worse than facing his own death.

Harry spends much of the book, consequently, with his teacher/ analyst Professor Lupin, learning how to conjure a Patronus Charm that will protect him from the dementors. Not surprisingly, Harry's Patronus is very much about his late father.

His meeting with Dumbledore after the bizarre climax of *Prisoner of Azkaban* is a return to the discussion in *Sorcerer's Stone* of death and our relationship with the dead who loved us. Harry admits to Dumbledore that he thought he saw his dead father save him from the dementor's kiss. Dumbledore's response is that the dead we love never "truly leave us" and that James Potter "is alive in you, Harry, and shows himself most plainly when you have need of him."[4]

We return here to the lesson we learned about love and death through Dumbledore at the end of the first book: that the love of the departed lives on in us as a protecting grace, and in this, the dead are never truly "departed." In Love, which is Christ, the saints are a "cloud of witnesses" ever encompassing those joined with him in his church (Hebrews 12:1).

DEATH IN *HARRY POTTER AND THE GOBLET OF FIRE*

We see a picture of this theme again in Harry's combat with Lord Voldemort at the end of *Goblet of Fire*. Lily and James Potter, via the "Priori Incantantem" effect, appear as shadowy echoes out of Voldemort's wand (in the company of his other victims). Harry's dad coaches him, comforts him, and after explaining to Harry how to escape, gives him the cue to go, attacking Voldemort with the other shadows in order to buy Harry the time he needs to get away. Not bad for a dead man who is not even a ghost.

But the end of *Goblet of Fire* is mostly about how to grieve. Cedric Diggory is murdered in Voldemort's black resurrection, and the community is stunned. Dumbledore puts on his Elisabeth Kübler-Ross hat and insists that Harry talk through his ordeal right away. He offers the answers that Harry needs in order to accept and recover from his experience, and then Dumbledore publicly acknowledges the heroism of the dead student in the Leaving Feast so the community has its closing ritual. (We learn how *not* to grieve from the house-elf Winkie, who chose to drink herself into oblivion and not share with anyone that her master, Barty Crouch Jr., was alive.)

DEATH IN *HARRY POTTER AND THE ORDER OF THE PHOENIX*

Alastor Moody shows Harry an old photo of the original Order of the Phoenix. In a spirit of nostalgia he relates how those pictured were almost all murdered by Death Eaters and Voldemort— and though he doesn't retell the story of their deaths, "Mad-Eye" Moody is sure to show Harry his dead parents. Harry is revolted by Moody's tactlessness. In the same chapter, while Moody watches, Harry sees Mrs. Weasly grieve for all her children and family (including Harry) when a Boggart reveals to her a vision of her worst fear: their deaths.

Moody's plan? I assume it was to remind the boy-man that a war must have casualties. Certainly Harry was temporarily sobered. He was in no way prepared for Sirius Black's death when it came, of course. And nothing Dumbledore said at the end of *Order of the Phoenix* made Black's death less of a senseless, agonizing loss to Harry.

DEATH IN *HARRY POTTER AND THE HALF-BLOOD PRINCE*

The death of Albus Dumbledore—the beloved Hogwarts headmaster, Harry's mentor, and the greatest wizard and alchemist of the age—is the climax of *Half-Blood Prince*. Whether he was murdered or already dead even before the novel begins is the subject of frenetic speculation and, no doubt, will continue to be until we have the final book to settle all arguments.[5] What we do know now is that Dumbledore, Harry's best example in life, leaves him the best example of how to die. The headmaster dies a death that is simultaneously:

- Heroic—He rushes to the Astronomy Tower when he sees the Dark Mark, despite knowing he is at death's door.
- Merciful—The headmaster uses his last strength to reveal gently to Draco Malfoy a lifesaving mercy and love unlike anything the boy could have expected from a man he was trying to kill.
- Selfless—Dumbledore, as he dies on the Tower turret, labors to help Draco, Harry, and Severus—and he does not make any effort to save himself. Even those former students, now Death Eaters, who have come to kill him are challenged and edified by his grace while dying.
- Fearless—The great alchemist clearly does not fear death, because he is both courteous to those taunting him and insistent on their good behavior. He acts as their host and teacher—and remains "upright" as long as possible—while he awaits his execution.
- Sacrificial—Albus could escape but allows Severus to "push him over the edge" to save Snape's life, which otherwise would have been lost because of the Unbreakable Vow.

Coupled with his actions in the cave (discussed in chapter 16 of this book), Albus Dumbledore's death is a loving, fearless, sacrificial death that testifies to life. Harry has a Christlike standard to take with him in his coming confrontation with Lord Voldemort.

We readers, like Harry at the end of *Half-Blood Prince*, can find a lot to hope for in Dumbledore's death and in the message of these books; namely, that death is not the end, that a soulless existence is worse than death, and that death can be transcended by love and the bond of blood. Let's look at these one at a time.

Death is not the end. Death is no joke in Harry Potter, certainly. Dumbledore tells us in *Goblet of Fire* that "no spell can re-awaken the dead," and so far, everyone who has bought the farm, on or off stage, has stayed dead. Harry tries to find a way to bring Sirius back as a ghost, but Nearly Headless Nick assures him at the very end of *Order of the Phoenix* that Sirius "will have . . . gone on." Only cowardly wizards like Nick, afraid of death, "choose to remain behind" as an "imprint of themselves."[6]

This shatters Harry—until he is reminded by Luna that they have evidence of an afterlife. In the Department of Mysteries (situated below the Ministry of Magic—which is already far underground) is the Death Chamber. At the center of a sunken theater-in-the-round with tiers of descending stone benches is a raised stone platform on which stands a broken, ancient stone archway. "The archway was hung with a tattered black curtain or veil, which, despite the complete stillness of the cold surrounding air, was fluttering very slightly as though it had just been touched."[7]

Harry and Luna hear voices behind the veil, though there is no one visible on the other side. When Sirius is killed in battle with Bellatrix Lestrange in the Death Chamber, he literally "passes through the veil," a traditional English idiom for dying. Luna reminds Harry that, yes, death is final, but the fact that they hear voices on the other side of the veil means there is good reason to hope for an afterlife.

A soulless existence is worse than death. If there is one single difference between Harry Potter and Voldemort, it is that Harry thinks there are worse things than dying. Voldemort reminds his supporters at his rebirthing party at the end of *Goblet of Fire:* "You know my goal—to conquer death." He claims to have taken "the steps" to "guard [himself] against mortal death" and "to have gone further than anybody along the path that leads to immortality."[8] As Voldemort shouts at Dumbledore in their wand-to-wand combat in *Order of the Phoenix*, "There is nothing worse than death, Dumbledore!"[9]

Voldemort, fearing death, pursues personal immortality through his horrible Horcruxes. He creates reservoirs in material objects for the splinters of his soul that have separated from the whole in the act of murder. The Dark Lord is merely a cartoon of fallen man; he asserts and seeks his advantage before others (a shadow of murder) and invests himself in temporal things and ideas (modern idolatry and materialism) to flee death and imagine himself immortal. Such a self-focused, unloving existence ironically separates him from the love of others and ultimately from Love himself, who is our life and hope of genuine immortality. Fleeing a human death, Voldemort becomes its nonliving, inhuman incarnation.

In contrast, when given Dumbledore's choice between what is good and what is easy, Harry always chooses the good—even though it means the probable loss of his life. He does so at the moment of crisis in every book.

What could be worse than death? A selfish life without truth, love, and beauty—a life on the Dark Side, chosen in fear of physical death, a life that is not really life at all. A physical life without a soul is what happens to a dementor's victim, as Professor Lupin explains to Harry in *Prisoner of Azkaban:* "You'll just—exist. As an empty shell. And your soul is gone forever . . . lost."[10]

The war taking shape between the forces of good and evil in the coming book is largely between those who think physical life (existence) is the greatest good and those who think what gives life meaning (the soul's ability to love and laugh) is more real and important than just what is visible (namely, continued physical existence). "To be carnally minded is death; but to be spiritually minded is life and peace" (Romans 8:6, KJV). Harry (like Saint Paul) knows that physical death is not the greatest evil; living a soulless existence in fear of death is the true death of the human spirit and the greater evil.

Death is transcended by love and the bond of blood. Death may not be anything at all. I don't mean to be cute. *Evil,* as defined by philosophers and many Christian thinkers, is not something existent in itself; rather, it's an absence or a negation. Death as an evil is life turning up missing from where it should be. How do we protect ourselves from this chasm? How do we transcend death?

As we have seen, Dumbledore tells Harry at the end of *Sorcerer's Stone* and *Prisoner of Azkaban* that his parents, through their love for him and his for them, are still alive in him. We learn in *Order of the Phoenix* that the sacrificial love of his mother is what has protected him from Voldemort his whole life.

Dumbledore calls the "ancient magic" he uses consequent to

Lily's sacrifice "the bond of blood." He places Harry with Lily's sister because her home is a place where Harry's mother's blood dwells. As Dumbledore puts it, "Her blood became your refuge."[11]

Dumbledore is not talking about a refuge in family blood, clearly; the Potter books (as shown in the previous chapter) deal extensively with the evil in families who think they deserve special privileges because of the purity of their blood. The refuge of blood Dumbledore is talking about is possible because of the sacrificial love of Harry's mom.

Does this idea of a refuge in blood sound familiar to you? It is probably because the idea of a blood refuge echoes in story form Christ's promise to his apostles that "whoso eateth my flesh, and drinketh my blood, hath eternal life; and I will raise him up at the last day" (John 6:54, KJV; see also Matthew 26:27-28; I Corinthians 11:24-25; Ephesians 1:7; and Hebrews 13:12, 20). His divine essence and sacrifice for us are necessary for our salvation and victory over death. Harry has the imaginative equivalent: freedom from death through the "bond of blood" magic that resulted from the loving sacrifice of Lily Potter.

Why does Harry need such a refuge? We learn in *Order of the Phoenix* that a boy of Harry's description was prophesied before his birth to be the coming vanquisher of the Dark Lord: "He will have power the Dark Lord knows not."[12] Voldemort learns of the prophecy, rightly or wrongly believes it is about Harry, and hunts him down. Lily Potter's sacrifice saves Harry as an infant and protects him in his first meetings with the Dark Lord and within the refuge of his aunt's home. But Voldemort hunts on.

Which brings us to the power Harry has that "the Dark Lord knows not." When Voldemort tells Dumbledore there is nothing worse than death, the headmaster tells him he is wrong.

"Indeed, your failure to understand that there are things much worse than death has always been your greatest weakness."[13]

Perhaps you scratched your head at this point in the story and asked yourself, "What could be worse than the absence of life?" Rowling tells us (through Dumbledore) that what is worse than an absence of life is an absence of love—and that love trumps death just as light overcomes darkness. Dumbledore describes the power of love as a transcendent force within Harry that is sufficient to vanquish the Dark Lord:

"There is a room in the Department of Mysteries," interrupted Dumbledore, "that is kept locked at all times. It contains a force that is at once more wonderful and more terrible than death, than human intelligence, than forces of nature. It is also, perhaps, the most mysterious of the many subjects for study that reside there. It is the power held within that room that you possess in such quantities and which Voldemort has not at all. That power took you to save Sirius tonight. That power saved you from possession by Voldemort, because he could not bear to reside in a body so full of the force that he detests. In the end, it mattered not that you could not close your mind. It was your heart that saved you."[14]

Harry and friends had tried to force this door with Sirius's knife in their adventure in the Department of Mysteries—but the force behind the door had melted the knife. Over Luna's objections, they choose to try another door and leave the power to save them all behind—until, as Dumbledore points out, Harry expels the possessing Voldemort by recalling his beloved Sirius. Voldemort, like Quirrell in *Sorcerer's Stone*, burns and flees.

Love is behind the door, love is the power that Voldemort cannot understand or endure, and it is love, the sacrificial love that saves Harry, which permeates Harry's heart and gives him a reflected part of its power.

DEATH AND THE CHRISTIAN MEANING OF HARRY POTTER

Rowling has told us a central theme of her books is death. Can we say that the treatment of this theme is an edifying one for Christians? Yes, we can. A quick review on what Christians know about death is in order.

The purpose of the incarnation of God was to destroy death by death. Love himself became a man, lived sinlessly, sacrificed himself in love for his creations, and blew a hole through the veil, figuratively speaking. With his death "the veil of the temple was rent," literally speaking (Matthew 27:51, KJV), and he opened for us passage to eternal life with him in God's eternal glory (also called his love and his mercy).

How do we participate in Christ's resurrection? How do we share in his victory for us over death? First, by living in love. All the moral virtues we have and good deeds we do are trash unless we have love, specifically his love (1 Corinthians 13). To use Rowling's language, when we "take refuge in the bond of blood"—which Christians know as the sacrificial blood of Christ on the cross—we are fortified in Love himself against death.

Paul teaches that "the wages of sin is death" (Romans 6:23). Death, in other words, is the life spent in selfish pursuit of advantage rather than with the God who is Life and Love himself. This pseudolife apart from God is a death worse than a physical death because it promises an eternity in darkness outside the glory of God. We experience true life when we choose against death and accept a life of love in resistance to selfishness and evil, spent in pursuit of communion with God, in victory over death made possible by the life and death-destroying resurrection of Christ.

Harry Potter doesn't lay out Christian doctrine explicitly, but Dumbledore comes close. Death, he tells us, "to the well-organized mind is just the next great adventure." Life is not a value to be pursued in itself; what value it does have we create by our choices—for the good over what is easy. Those who love us live on in us after their death because of this love, a love which is their immortality and which protects us—the Love which is Christ. Dumbledore teaches Harry not to fear death as much as a life without love, which is the real death.

The *wow!* of Rowling's presentation of this theme is our vicarious experience of dying heroically in resistance to evil with Harry in every book, then rising from the dead with him to talk with Dumbledore and those we love. This shared resurrection in *Sorcerer's Stone*, in case you resist the Easter parallel, comes after three days.[15] Rowling has us share in the spoils of a life spent in love and resistance to darkness by this cathartic death and resurrection—and it is the great joy, relief, and lesson of each book. Death is not final. Death has been overcome by Love himself.

Again, when I am asked if I think these books are safe for people (especially children) to read, I do not hesitate. Yes, I think these books are safe, and beyond that, they let us experience Love's victory over death in story form.

8

THE QUESTION
OF IDENTITY

*Harry defines himself through
choices, change, and destiny.*

Choice is the human ability to decide between two options.[1] If this
faculty is well trained, a person is able to discriminate or choose
well between options of good and evil, right and wrong, advantage
and disadvantage. In each of the Harry Potter stories, we're able to
see just what constitutes "good choosing."

The first dimension of choice is the implicit level. Harry makes
two types of choices in every book—about what sort of person he
is and about what to do in a crisis—and he consistently chooses
what is right over what is easy.

Let's look at the choices Harry makes—choices that will define
who he is. In each decision, Harry has the option of loyalty to a
high and difficult standard versus personal advantage. He chooses
(with one exception that has heavy consequences) loyalty to the
good.

- In *Sorcerer's Stone*, Harry asks not to be put in Slytherin House, though Draco Malfoy and the Sorting Hat point to Slytherin as his path to power.
- At the same time, he chooses to be friends with Ron and Hermione—one poor, the other unpopular and of questionable lineage, despite being advised (again by Draco) to avoid hanging out with "riffraff."
- In *Chamber of Secrets*, Harry professes his loyalty to Dumbledore at the risk of being murdered by Riddle/ Voldemort, Dumbledore's enemy.
- In *Prisoner of Azkaban*, Harry chooses to spare Pettigrew, who betrayed Harry's parents to their murderer, out of loyalty to his understanding of what his father would have wanted.
- In *Goblet of Fire*, Harry refuses to reconcile with Ron, despite loneliness and friendship for Ron, in loyalty to the truth.
- Later in the same book, Harry withstands persecution by the media, unabashed again because of his commitment to standing with what is true over what others think.
- In *Order of the Phoenix*, Harry chooses the easy way (*not* to study Occlumency with Snape and before bed), and the consequence is Sirius's coming to the Department of Mysteries to rescue Harry—and dying in battle.
- In *Half-Blood Prince*, Harry chooses to ignore Dumbledore's unqualified trust in Severus Snape and Ron and Hermione's skepticism about Draco being the youngest Death Eater in favor of his "age-old" prejudice against the Slytherins. We will see the consequences in the next and last book.

These internal choices are significant, and they are paired in each book with a life-or-death decision. Each choice occurs as the result of a crisis in which Harry must choose between what is safe and easy for him versus resisting evil at risk of his life. He chooses each time to do the right, dangerous thing. Consider the following life-or-death decisions:

- In *Sorcerer's Stone*, Harry chooses to pass Fluffy and enter the trapdoor in order to keep the Stone from Snape and Voldemort.
- In *Chamber of Secrets*, he opts to search for the Chamber in order to find Ron's sister Ginny, and in the Chamber he elects to fight Riddle against all odds.
- In *Prisoner of Azkaban*, Harry dives in front of Peter Pettigrew, saving him from Lupin and Black, who have wands drawn to kill him for betraying Lily and James Potter to Voldemort.
- In *Goblet of Fire*, Harry chooses to warn Cedric of a giant spider about to attack him (though that would have cleared his way to victory—and the spider turns on Harry!). He also chooses to resist and attack Voldemort in the graveyard—again, against all odds.
- In *Order of the Phoenix*, Harry "learns" in a dream that Sirius is being tortured by Death Eaters and rushes to his rescue.
- In *Half-Blood Prince*, Harry learns almost simultaneously of the mission to find the cave Horcrux and of a man who is celebrating in the Room of Requirement, which he rightly assumes is a sign that Malfoy has completed his assignment. Harry chooses to go with Dumbledore—and to "call up" Dumbledore's army to patrol the castle in their absence.

Harry's choices deliver the implicit message "Do the hard, right thing; don't take the easy, advantageous route." What does Dumbledore teach us about choice in his discussions with Harry and others? You guessed it: "Your choices are what matter" and "Choose what is right over what is easy."

In *Chamber of Secrets*, Harry is confronted repeatedly with suggestions that he is somehow akin to the Dark Lord. He learns at the end, from Voldemort and Dumbledore, that there is some truth in that. Harry then asks Dumbledore if he should have been put in Slytherin House, where (Harry believes) the Sorting Hat thought he belonged. Dumbledore responds that while Harry has much in common with Voldemort and the Slytherins, he is different from the bad guys largely because he *asked* not to be put in Slytherin House. "It is our choices, Harry, that show who we truly are, far more than our abilities" (chapter 18).

Dumbledore reemphasizes the relative importance of our choices compared with our birthright in *Goblet of Fire*. Confronting the stuffed-shirt Minister of Magic, he bares Fudge's prejudice by pointing to the fate of Barty Crouch Jr. "Your dementor has just destroyed the last remaining member of a pure-blood family as old as any—and see what that man chose to make of his life!"[2]

Your life is of value only if you choose the good over what is easy and evil. Dumbledore drives this point home in Churchill-like cadences to the assembled Hogwarts student body in the conclusion of his tribute to Cedric Diggory when he says, "Remember if the time should come when you have to make a choice between what is right and what is easy, remember what happened to a boy who was good and kind and brave, because he strayed across the path of Lord Voldemort."[3]

So we have the *implicit* treatment of choice in the choices Harry makes, and we have the *explicit* dimension in Dumbledore's talks on choice. Harry is often forced to make these difficult choices during the scenes of greatest drama, when we are most engaged in the story. In this way, we identify with Harry and make the choice with him, usually amazed at our own virtue.

In her treatment of choice Rowling engages us not in the choosing per se (as it was when "dying" with Harry) but in the goodness we experience as we choose the harder, virtuous, self-sacrificing option with Harry. C. S. Lewis called this "training in the Stock Responses" and thought it the responsibility of the better writer. Rowling stands with Lewis in using her art to assist our growth in virtue. And her readers like that. A lot. We participate imaginatively with the characters when they make good choices—and this reading experience positively influences the decision making in our own lives. Sort of like vitamins for the soul.

Choices aren't that big a deal, of course, except in the context of change or personal transformation. Dumbledore chides Fudge for not understanding that it is choice, not blood, that shapes the human person—and Draco Malfoy is always telling Harry the same thing.[4] Even the bad guys understand that your choices shape who you become. Choices we make both reflect the character we have and shape the character we will have. This is the same idea as keeping your house clean; it reflects the value you give order, and it shapes and confirms this priority in your life.

Now that we have discussed choice in Harry Potter, let's move on to a look at the consequences of our choices, that is, what we become: our changes and transformations.

CHANGE IN HARRY POTTER

Transfiguration is a required course in the Hogwarts curriculum. *Transfiguration* comes from the Latin *trans*, meaning "across" (hence "motion, change"), and *figura*, meaning "form, appearance, shape"— in other words, "shape changing." Young wizards and witches at Hogwarts are taught from the first year on the basics of turning beetles into buttons, up to the advanced magic (not with teacher approval, it seems) of "turning [your] friend into a badger."[5] Even though the Transfigurations Masters we meet in the stories are usually good guys, not all shape-changers are good!

There is, for example, a rather nasty creature called a Boggart that we meet in *Prisoner of Azkaban* that takes on the appearance of what a person fears most. It can be dispersed by a Riddikulus Charm and laughter—humor is a valuable weapon in fighting fear and evil.

One of the more poetic aspects of Transfiguration is that those who take the shape of animals become animals that are metaphors for their human characters. When Moody punishes Malfoy for attacking Harry when his back is turned, the sneaky and rodent-like Draco becomes a ferret that Moody bounces up and down with his wand. Hagrid tries to turn Dudley into a pig but only succeeds in giving him a curly pig's tail because, as he explains, Dudley is "so much like a pig there wasn't much left ter do."[6] The obnoxious and nosy reporter Rita Skeeter, of course, becomes a bug for the purpose of eavesdropping as an (illegal and unregistered) animagus.

If Harry's choices are good and good choices mean good changes, then we should see Harry changing via his choices and experiences from a child to a more mature, in-control, self-monitoring "human animal" (if you will) over the course of each year at Hogwarts. Not as exciting as watching Malfoy change into a ferret perhaps (if his choices seem to be confirming him in that role), but Harry's changes should be almost as dramatic. In fact, they are:

- When we meet Harry in *Sorcerer's Stone* he is a victim of his stepfamily's abuses and seemingly has no heritage. He has become, by book's end, a victor in battle against the Dark

Lord and the heir of his family's legacy. How? It is through his heroic choices, in which he chooses the good over his personal gain.

- *Chamber of Secrets*, too, opens with Harry literally and figuratively a prisoner; the Dursleys have locked him in his room, and he is moored in his own self-doubts and self-pity. He saves Ginny from her enchantment by the Dark Lord and escapes the Chamber at the end of the book on the wings of a phoenix, in every sense a free man. This transformation from prisoner to liberator is again a function of his choosing what is right rather than what is easy.

- In *Prisoner of Azkaban*, Harry's transformation is more profound than in any other book in the series until *Order of the Phoenix*.

Prisoner of Azkaban opens with Harry not at all in control of his passions. Vernon Dursley's sister, Aunt Marge, patronizes Harry as an unwelcome burden on her brother and at last insults him and his parents as an example of bad blood and poor breeding. Marge is a bulldog fancier, and given her name and the bulldog's being to Britain what the eagle is to America, I have to suspect she is a rather transparent caricature of Margaret Thatcher and her uncharitable opinions about dole recipients.

Harry's response? He tries some self-control techniques to ignore her but of course fails. He has too many unresolved feelings and unanswered questions about his parents' death and especially about his dad to suffer Aunt Marge gladly. In a rage (and without a wand), Harry makes this woman, so full of herself, into a three-dimensional picture of her character by "blowing her up"—not as a bomb blows up, but as a

balloon. Aunt Marge and her bulldog point to Margaret
Thatcher and John Bull patriots whom Rowling believes
were self-inflated monsters.

Harry experiences the death of his parents again and
again in *Prisoner of Azkaban,* courtesy of the dementors and
a Boggart. He learns from his analyst, "Dr." Lupin, how
to fight off the depression and despair brought on by these
nasties. When he learns in the Shrieking Shack of Pettigrew's
Judas-like betrayal, he has been changed so much by his
choices in therapy and his consequent enlightenment that
not only does he refrain from attacking Pettigrew, but he
risks his own life to save Wormtail.

He has transformed from a passionate child rushing to
judgment and punishment on Privet Drive to a young adult
capable of great discernment and semidivine mercy. Both
Dumbledore and Black comment that at last Harry is "truly
[his] father's son."[7] He has become not really an orphan but
a living image of his father.

- Harry begins *Goblet of Fire* as a boy understandably concerned
  about what others think and say about him. His experiences
  and choices following a fight with Ron and an article in the
  Daily Prophet transform him into a mature young man more
  interested in "being" than "seeming." His personal integrity
  and emotional maturity allow him to rise above popularity
  concerns or fear of slander.

  When Rita Skeeter's second article about Harry in the
  Daily Prophet appears on the morning of the last Triwizard
  task (titled "Harry Potter: Disturbed and Dangerous"),
  Harry shrugs off her portrayal of him as a troubled mental
  defective. " 'Gone off me a bit, hasn't she?' said Harry lightly,
  folding up the paper."[8] This accomplishment is in a way

more remarkable than his successes in the Triwizard Tournament tasks and is the foundation of his ability to fight Voldemort to a draw at the Dark Lord's rebirthing party. The primary characters in Harry Potter, although mostly children, are never especially childish; by the end of *Goblet of Fire*, Harry has transformed into a real he-man of sacrificial virtue and is nearly a superhero.

- In the opening of *Order of the Phoenix*, Harry is a caged animal who looks outside himself for his bearings. He digs in garbage cans for newspapers and fights to listen to the evening news for some word about Voldemort's return. By the end of the book, the exterior world has stripped Harry of everything about himself because of the choices he makes to speak the truth and be loyal to his friends. Though he never learns the introverted skill of Occlumency, his losses through the year (and especially the death of his godfather, Sirius) turn him inside out from year's start. By the end of the book, Harry has learned to look to his heart for his bearings and to the world for very little.

- When we meet Harry in *Half-Blood Prince*, he is half-asleep, "looking through a glass darkly," waiting for Dumbledore, and very much in doubt that Albus will come (though the headmaster had written in no uncertain terms that he would come). Harry testifies to Scrimgeour at story's end, after Dumbledore's funeral, that he is a "Dumbledore man, through and through" and that he feels his mentor's presence in death more nearly than he did while living.

One aside here. As we talked about earlier, much of the imagery of change in the Potter novels springs from the tradition of alchemical symbolism in English literature. Every Potter book ends with a superheated crucible scene in which the characters reveal themselves and transform into greater or lesser people (see the chapters on individual books for more on this). Dissolution, purification, and perfection, the three stages of the alchemical Great Work (and of changing the human soul from lead to gold), are reflected in Harry's transformations.

Perhaps the formula of "good, hard choices make good people" strikes you as a little simplistic, leaving out as it does both ideas of fate or destiny and even the seeming arbitrariness of who is born into which families (the big "Sorting Hat"). This "fate or free will" question hangs over English literature. As it is often posed, the fate/ free will question goes something like this: God sees all and knows all—past, present, and future—so in what sense can human beings be said to act freely? If all human action is foreordained in God's knowledge, this contradicts the idea of human freedom and God's revelation that he longs for our freewill decision to live in communion with his divine will. In less theological language, the question has been posed as a matter of our programming. Are we simply programmed machines of matter and energy, designed to reproduce our specific programming? From this perspective, even acts of self-sacrifice are understood as defenses of the local gene pool; free will and altruism are fictitious concepts, no more, no less.

This is no small matter. You read every day or hear from friends about how circumstances outside someone's control (read "fate," "destiny," or even "providence") *determine* a person's actions and character. Perhaps they grew up poor in a bad neighborhood or with parents who neglected and beat them. The Harry Potter books have a different, sobering emphasis. Whereas our popular culture often excuses people based on their circumstances, these books raise the question of responsibility for our actions and point out that our choices have moral significance.

The Harry Potter books take aim at the "you're as good or bad as your programming" position. Again and again, we see that it's our choices that shape us; if we make the good, hard choices against evil, we will become a better person.

But it's clear that even Rowling's characters are born with a destiny. As hinted strongly in the first books and revealed outright in *Order of the Phoenix*, Harry has been born with the mother lode of responsibility. In three stages, we've come to think of Harry as more than the sum of his choices.

First, it was the King Arthur references. From the opening of *Sorcerer's Stone*, the parallels with the legend of King Arthur are remarkable. Harry and Arthur are both orphans hidden and protected by grand wizards. Harry's being shown respect by the chess king in *Sorcerer's Stone* points to his innate royalty. Even the magical sky ceiling above the Great Hall at Hogwarts is an exact copy of the enchanted ceiling above the round table at Camelot. And just as Arthur pulls a sword from a stone to show he is the rightful heir to the throne, so Harry pulls the sword of Godric Gryffindor from the Sorting Hat in *Chamber of Secrets*. Harry's love for (and romance with, in *Half-Blood Prince*) Ginny Weasley, whose first name is "Ginevra," a variant of "Guinevere," is just icing on the Arthurian cake.

Second, we have the Heir of Gryffindor references. Besides Harry being called "a true Gryffindor" by Dumbledore at the end of *Chamber of Secrets* and the red and gold sparks that fly from Harry's wand involuntarily when he's angry,[9] the Gryffindor/Slytherin opposition through the books points to Harry as Heir of Gryffindor.

Both Harry and Voldemort are not from pure-blood families. Both Harry and Voldemort grew up as orphans in painful living situations. Both have qualities in common: "Parseltongue—resourcefulness—determination—a certain disregard for rules."[10]

Tom Riddle says, "We even *look* something alike."[11] Harry and Voldemort are mirror-reflection doppelgängers; the apposition of Harry with Voldemort, the Heir of Slytherin, throughout the books suggests Voldemort knows Harry is Heir of Gryffindor. Gryffindor means "golden griffin" (golden eagle/lion) and is a pointer to Christ, the King of heaven and earth (see chapter 9). Harry, as Heir of Gryffindor, is clearly more than your average boy wizard or just the product of his environment and choices.

Third and last are the revelations of the prophecy in *Order of the Phoenix*. We've already seen that Harry (and/or Neville) was prophesied before his birth to be the coming vanquisher of Voldemort, complete with a power the Dark Lord "knows not." The vanquisher's life is not one he can choose to disregard; the prophecy says in detail that the Dark Lord and his vanquisher have a kill-or-be-killed relationship that isn't to be ducked. Like King Arthur, Harry, as Heir of Gryffindor and prophesied vanquisher of the Dark Lord—is a boy with a remarkable "career track"!

So the question, now that we know that Harry was born into this giant-sized destiny, is how important are his choices after all? Wasn't he born to his difficult, heroic choices the same way Malfoy was born to his nasty Slytherin decisions? Isn't his seeming free will just a function of his predestined programming?

Rowling takes aim at this view, both in interviews (as she gave at the publication of *Half-Blood Prince*) and in the narrative of *Half-Blood Prince* itself. In this book, Dumbledore's big teaching moment comes before the adventure in the cave and the Astronomy Tower. He enlightens Harry about the difference between fatalism—that is, a future predetermined by God or circumstances to which one is resigned—and human freedom, which is choosing as best as one can to meet one's destiny heroically. Here is Harry's reaction:

He understood at last what Dumbledore had been trying to tell him. It was, he thought, the difference between being dragged into the arena to face a battle to the death and walking into the arena with your head held high. Some perhaps, would say that there was little to choose between the two ways, but Dumbledore knew—and so do I, thought Harry with a rush of fierce pride, and so did my parents—that there was all the difference in the world.[12]

If the reader wants to believe in an existential fatalism, something like Harry sitting at the window staring into the darkness and doubting the arrival of his deliverance, rather than in moral virtue and heroic choice of the good, that reader is fighting the tide of Rowling's message. The human heart thrills in resonance to Harry's heroic decisions—decisions made (until Dumbledore's revelations at the end of *Order of the Phoenix*) without knowledge of his destiny. Readers around the world share his programming, it seems, to the tune of more than 300 million copies of Harry's stories being sold. If this is only a matter of programming, there seems a prevalent programming in the human person for sacrificial, altruistic, loving service that loyalty to the local gene pool does not explain. Why do we thrill to Harry's choices if they're just a function of his being the boy born to be "king"?[13]

The answer to this question brings us to the Christian meaning of choice and change in Harry Potter. Harry, it turns out, has a larger-than-life destiny (vanquish Voldemort; save the world). But he can only realize this destiny by making the right choices and becoming the sort of person—an embodiment of love, the power the Dark Lord knows not—able to defeat the Dark Lord.

Yes, Harry has a destiny, but his freewill choices are what will make the difference between his realizing his prophesied end or not. Why does our heart thrill to this message? Because we, too, have a prophesied end in which our choices every day, choices for or against our becoming more loving people and more like God, are the deal makers or breakers. We are born as the images of God, created for an eternal life in his presence. We have a choice, however, because of the free will we enjoy from him: We can become images in the *likeness* of God by choosing love over death and sharing in the resurrection of Love himself—or we can choose the easy road of advantage and personal comfort (a metaphor in our heart for immunity to pain and death). It is our daily choices that make this difference: image or likeness? Love or death?

Reading Harry Potter is an edifying lift and support for human beings because we have a designed end in God. By reading these books and identifying with the hero's good choices, we get a boost via our imaginations to do the right thing in difficult circumstances ourselves. Our circumstances may make these choices relatively hard or obvious, but Harry's choices point us to the ones we must make in order to realize our prophesied destinies as a "royal priesthood" (I Peter 2:9) and heirs of the *real* Golden Griffin.

9

EVIDENCE OF
THINGS UNSEEN

The symbols in Potterdom are powerful
pointers to Christian reality.

Do you groan when you read the word *symbolism?* If so, I bet I
know why. You had a high school English teacher like mine who
made sure you "got" the symbolism in everything you read—from
the great White Whale in *Moby Dick* to the all-seeing billboard eye-
glasses in *The Great Gatsby.* Problem was, she never explained how
symbolism worked or why these supposedly great writers were
spending so much time hiding what they meant behind silly images
and metaphors. I figured it was just another adult game for writers
and literature teachers to enjoy.

Boy, was I wrong. I will go so far as to say that this chapter on
symbolism is the most important chapter in this book in terms of
our ability to understand the popularity of Harry Potter, to understand the Christian meaning of the books, and even to understand
the right reasons for Christians to object to stories their children
are reading. Once we understand symbols we can better understand

what it means to be human. As creatures made in "the image of God" (Genesis 1:26-27), we are three-dimensional symbols, in time and space, of the Trinity.

The world we live in is incomprehensible except in light of symbols. As Martin Lings, tutorial student and friend of C. S. Lewis, wrote:

> *There is no traditional doctrine which does not teach that the world is the world of symbols, inasmuch as it contains nothing which is not a symbol. A man should therefore understand at least what that means, not only because he has to live in the herebelow but also and above all because without such understanding he would fail to understand himself, he being the supreme and central symbol in the terrestrial state.*[1]

Symbolism is not just an English major's thing—it's a human thing.

Let's start by ridding ourselves of some of the mistaken ideas we may have been taught about symbolism. Symbolism is not something "standing in" for something else, a tit-for-tat allegory. An allegory is a story or word picture in which something existing on earth is represented by another earthly character or image. Some critics, for example, have written that *The Lord of the Rings* is an allegory of the Second World War, with Sauron and the forces of darkness standing in for the Axis powers while the Fellowship of the Ring and other white hats represent the Allies. As readers, we don't interpret allegories as much as we translate them; allegories, unlike symbols, are just a translation of one story into another language or story. Neither are symbols simply signs, or at least they are not like street signs, which are simple representations for earthly instructions or things (such as Stop or Deer Crossing).

Literary characters and stories are not necessarily symbolic.

Great novels like *The Pilgrim's Progress* are allegorical both in regard to their characters and story line. Christian's journey in *Progress* is a detailed picture of events and people met on every Christian's earthly journey. The men that he meets—I think immediately of "Mr. Worldly WiseMan" (a great stand-in for television talking heads)—are cardboard cutouts of people we meet every day who support or obstruct us in our passage to the heavenly kingdom.

Many stories that are symbolic, however, are often mistakenly explained (and dismissed) as allegories. Please note that little else disturbed C. S. Lewis and J. R. R. Tolkien as much as critical explanation of their fiction as "allegorical" (as in the WWII analogy). The reason their books touch us so deeply and have endured in popularity as long as they have is because of their symbolic meaning.

Symbols, rather than analogies for other earthly events, are transparencies through which we see greater realities than we can see on earth (see 1 Corinthians 13:12 and 2 Corinthians 3:18). The ocean as it stretches to the distant horizon is a symbol of the infinite power and breadth of God. In seeing the one, we can sense the other. The ocean as a body of water has no power in itself to stir the heart; it's just an oversized bathtub. But as a symbol of God, a way of seeing the unseeable, it can take our breath away or bring tears to our eyes.

Symbols are windows, too, through which otherworldly realities (powers, graces, and qualities) intrude into the world. As Lings wrote, this is the traditional understanding of Creation—that all earthly things and events testify to "the invisible things of him from the creation of the world" (Romans 1:20, KJV). This testimony includes the power of natural beauty and grandeur (think of mountain ranges, a field of flowers, or a lion on the savanna). It also includes sacred art, architecture, and liturgy, which are by definition symbolic in their portrayal of greater-than-earthly realities.[2]

Christ, of course, speaks in story symbols, too, through his parables. He knows we cannot understand the truth as it exists, so he wraps these truths in edifying stories or windows we can look through in order to experience some likeness of truth. "These things have I spoken unto you in proverbs: but the time cometh, when I shall no more speak unto you in proverbs, but I shall shew you plainly of the Father" (John 16:25, KJV). Until we see things "face to face" (I Corinthians 13:12), though, we have symbols to understand ourselves and Creation.

Man, as an image and likeness of God, is a living symbol—both in the sense of transparency through which we look and of an opening through which God enters the world. Man is created in the image of God so that the world will reverence the God who cannot be seen (see I John 4:20 and the sequence of the Great Commandments in Mark 12:30-31). He also is designed to be a vehicle of God's grace, power, and love intruding into the world of time and space. The tragedy of man's fall is that, because most people no longer believe they are symbols of God, shaped in his likeness, it is more difficult to see God in our neighbor, and the world is often denied access to God through his chosen vessel.

We are still moved, however, by the symbols in nature and the symbols that we experience in story form. This is the power of myth: that we can experience invisible spiritual realities and truths greater than visible, material things in story form. Tolkien described Christianity as the "True Myth," the ultimate intrusion of God into the world through his incarnation as Jesus of Nazareth. Tolkein's explanation of this idea was instrumental in C. S. Lewis's conversion to Christianity; it is this understanding of the purpose and power of story that gives his fiction its depth, breadth, and height.

Symbols in stories, just as the symbols in nature, sacred art, and edifying myths, are able to put us in contact with a greater reality than what we can sense directly. They do this through our imagination. The power of Lewis's and Tolkien's writing is found in their profound symbolism; *The Lord of the Rings* is not a strained allegory or retelling of WWII but a dynamic symbol of the cosmic struggle between good and evil of which WWII was also but a real-world representation.

WHAT THIS MEANS FOR UNDERSTANDING HARRY POTTER

Knowing that symbols are points of passage between this world and the greater world "above"—and "within"—us explains a lot about Harry Potter and Potter-mania. Magic, for example, is not demonic or contrary to Scripture when used (as it is in Harry Potter) as a symbol of the miraculous power of God that men as images of God are designed to have (see John 14:12 and chapter 1 of this book).

Books that are rich in symbolism necessarily support a Christian worldview. The difference between believers and atheists or agnostics is that the secular crowd does not believe that anything exists beyond what can be sensed or measured. Everything is a this-worldly quantity. Christians understand the world to be a shadow of the reality of its Creator and that this greater reality—God—is rightly the focus of our lives. Symbolic literature requires—and celebrates—this otherworldly perspective that magically undermines the worldly, atheistic, and materialist perspective of our times.

This explains, too, why books that are rich in specifically Christian imagery and symbols are as powerful and popular as they are. Tertullian said that "all souls are Christian souls," and Augustine echoed him in writing that "our hearts are restless 'til they rest in Thee." Since we as human beings are designed for the Christian revelation, stories that retell the Great Story satisfy the longing we are hardwired to feel and answer.

Unlike most contemporary novels, which portray realistic morals or earthbound allegories, Harry Potter is very much a myth pointing to the True Myth. Take, for instance, lead characters Harry, Ron, and Hermione. I already explained how Harry's two friends are ciphers for the "quarreling couple" of alchemy, but there is a more profound symbolism the trio, Snape's "Dream Team," make up.

What's great about this usage is that you've seen it before. Take a look at this chart:

Work	Body (Desire)	Mind (Will)	Spirit (Heart)
Fyodor Dostoyevsky's *Brothers Karamazov*	Dmitri Karamazov	Ivan Karamazov	Alyosha Karamazov
C. S. Lewis's *Narnia Chronicles*	Edmund Pevensie	Peter Pevensie	Lucy Pevensie
J. R. R. Tolkien's *Lord of the Rings*	Smeagol (Gollum)	Sam Gamgee	Frodo Baggins
Gene Roddenberry's *Star Trek*	Bones	Spock	Kirk
George Lucas's *Star Wars*	Han Solo	Princess Leia	Luke Skywalker
J. K. Rowling's *Harry Potter*	Ron Weasley	Hermione Granger	Harry Potter

Writers as different as Dostoyevsky and Tolkien, television producers and moviemakers, have all used this particular symbolism—because it works. Man is most obviously an image of God in that his soul is three parts; it has three faculties or powers symbolizing the three persons of the Godhead.[3] We call these powers "belly," "head," and "chest," or more commonly "body," "mind," and "spirit."[4]

Rather than try to show how these three principal faculties respond to situations as a sum in every character, artists can create

characters that represent *one* of these faculties and show in story
how these powers of the soul relate to one another. Every one of
the original *Star Trek* television shows, for example, was a psychic
drama of Kirk (spirit) leading Spock (mind) and Bones (body)
against some outer-space adversary.

Harry, Ron, and Hermione can easily be connected with their
corresponding faculties. Ron is the physical, comfort-focused com-
plainer; Hermione, the thinker; and Harry, the heroic heart that
leads the company.

So what? To understand the purpose and power of this literary
model, take a moment to think of Harry, Ron, and Hermione's
relationships—when they work and when they don't. Harry is
clearly in charge. Hermione is the best thinker. Ron is the cheer-
leader and flag-waver (in his best moments). When they follow
Harry's lead in line—Harry, Hermione, Ron—all goes well. Think
of their assault on the obstacles leading to the Stone or their team-
work to get to the Chamber of Secrets: amazing work for preteens.

But when the team breaks down and the players don't play their
roles or won't play them in obedience to Harry, things go wrong in
the worst way. In the first six books, this has happened twice, both
times because Ron, low man in the hierarchy of faculties, takes the
wrong role.

In *Prisoner of Azkaban,* Ron takes the lead position. He gets into
a bitter fight with Hermione about her decision to tell Professor
McGonagall about Harry's broom and then about her pet cat's
seeming to have made a meal of his pet rat. As Hagrid points out,
a broom and a rat are hardly reason to throw off a friend, especially
a friend in need; but no matter, Harry follows Ron's passionate
cues and stops speaking to Hermione. Harry also decides to go to
Hogsmeade on Ron's advice and against Hermione's pleas—and
narrowly misses being expelled. Lupin shames Harry; Ron comes

to his senses, apologizes to Harry, and they reconcile with Hermione—with Ron again in a place of service to his friends.

In *Goblet of Fire*, Ron breaks entirely with Harry out of jealousy and meanness of spirit when Harry is chosen by the Goblet to be a school champion. Ron is pathetic on his own, and Harry misses his friend terribly, but he learned his lesson in *Prisoner of Azkaban*: the heart following selfish, spiteful passions gets you nowhere good, fast. Ron returns to the fold after the first Triwizard task, the danger of which seems to have jerked him back into remembrance of his rightful place in Harry's service.

We should remember that it is Hermione who almost has nervous breakdowns during her time apart from Harry and Ron and during Ron's break with Harry. This is not feminine weakness, but rather a picture of the fragility of an intellect that is disembodied and heartless. Part of Hermione's brilliance is her determined dependence on her friends; she understands that her jewel intelligence is glorious in its right setting and almost inhuman on its own (remember Hermione at the beginning of *Sorcerer's Stone?*).

In *Order of the Phoenix*, Harry is separated from Ron and Hermione by virtue of their being selected as house prefects. Ron and Hermione both flourish as they take on responsibilities independent of Harry—and at the same time, their appreciation for him and their friendship grows apace. The trio's love for one another and our identification with them makes their hard times with each other the most painful parts of the stories—and their reconciliation the most joyous. We become aligned in this identification—spirit to mind to body—and feel strangely upright and all right for the change.

Good literature trains us in the "stock responses" and lets us see and pattern ourselves after the right alignment of the soul's powers. When our desires are in line with our will, and both will and desire are obedient to directions from the heart or spirit, we are in operation the way we were designed to be. Turn this upside down, though, so that will and spirit answer to the desires (as the commercials in our desire-driven culture would have it), and you have a wreck-in-the-making. The human person isn't designed to be belly-led, as Scripture, history, and experience all testify (see Romans 16:18 and Philippians 3:19, and visit any one of the addiction recovery programs in your neighborhood).

MYTHICAL BEASTS IN HARRY POTTER

For most of us, the connection between an animal and its symbolic quality is pretty clear. A dog embodies and radiates the virtue of loyalty; a cat, feminine beauty and grace; a lion, power and majesty; an eagle, freedom; and a horse, nobility.

The animals in Harry Potter are not your conventional domestic pets or zoo beasts. Rowling has a rich imagination and a special fascination for fantastic beasts; she has even written a Hogwarts "schoolbook," *Fantastic Beasts and Where to Find Them,* cataloging her favorites, A–Z. Are these products of her imagination symbols in the way eagles and lions are symbols?

Yes and no. No, I don't think a fictional lion (say, the one that occurs throughout the Potter books on the banners of Gryffindor House or the lion Aslan in Lewis's Chronicles of Narnia) has the same power to suggest "majesty" as a real lion on the savanna. One works through the sense of vision and the other through the imagination. But, yes, if the fictional beast is capably depicted, both contain the quality that makes the lion regal and stirs the heart.

Many of the animals in Harry Potter are Rowling's own inventions (although the acromantula reminds Tolkien fans of the giant spider Shelob and of the den of spiders in *The Hobbit*). However, let's focus on traditional symbols from European literature because of the wealth of references that support the interpretation of their supernatural qualities. If there is a single giveaway of the Christian meaning in Harry Potter, it is in the uniform meaning of the symbols. The magical creatures and figures we will look at more closely are the griffin, the unicorn, the phoenix, the stag, the centaur, the hippogriff, the philosopher's stone, and the red lion. Each is a traditional symbol of arts and letters used to point to the qualities and person of Christ.

The Griffin

I've found only one mention of a griffin per se in the Harry Potter books, and it is a detail mentioned in connection to Dumbledore's office. Professor McGonagall is bringing Harry there in *Chamber of Secrets* after he has been discovered next to the petrified forms of Justin Finch-Fletchley and Nearly Headless Nick: "Harry saw a gleaming oak door ahead, with a brass knocker in the shape of a griffin."[5]

The griffin is described in *Fantastic Beasts* as having "the front legs and head of a giant eagle, but the body and hind legs of a lion."[6] It is an important symbol in the Potter series, though only mentioned once, because "Harry's House, Gryffindor, literally means 'golden griffin' in French (*or* is French for 'gold')."[7] So spell it "Griffin d'or." As Harry is considered a "true Gryffindor" in Dumbledore's estimation,[8] you can put a bet on there being great significance in the meaning of golden griffin for the identity of Harry Potter.

How does a beast that is half lion and half eagle symbolize Jesus Christ? Two ways. First, Christ is the God-man, so double-natured symbols are a natural match for him. More important, though, is that the two natures here are the lion and eagle. A beast that is half "king of the heavens" (eagle) and half "king of the earth" (lion) points to the God-man in his role as King of heaven and earth.[9]

The Unicorn

Harry first meets a unicorn in the Forbidden Forest under the worst of conditions. The unicorn is dying or dead; Voldemort, as something like a snake, is drinking its blood, which "tonic" curses the drinker but keeps him alive.[10] Unicorns pop up again in Ms. Grubberly Plank's and Hagrid's Care of Magical Creatures classes.[11]

I remember as a young boy being taken to the Cloisters, a New York museum of medieval art in an authentic castle brought stone by stone from Europe. The highlight of the trip was the tapestries—specifically the unicorn tapestries. The guide told us that the unicorn was the symbol of Christ preferred by the weavers of these giant pieces. Though I was a child of no special faith (or sensitivity), I was moved by the images of the unicorn being chased, captured, and resting its head on a virgin's lap.

A check in *Strong's Concordance to the Bible* reveals mentions of unicorns in the Old Testament books of Deuteronomy, Numbers, Job, Psalms, and Isaiah.[12] One Harry Potter guidebook comments that "these references, to some scholars indicate that the unicorn is actually a symbol of Christ."[13] Scholars of symbolism as diverse as Carl Jung and Narnia expert Paul Ford confirm this interpretation of the pure white animal whose single horn symbolizes the "invincible strength of Christ."[14]

As we'll see in the chapter on *Harry Potter and the Sorcerer's Stone*, the unicorn as a symbol of Christ is essential in understanding the meaning of the dramatic scene in the Forbidden Forest.

The Phoenix

My flat-out favorite beastie in Rowling's menagerie is Fawkes the phoenix, Dumbledore's pet. Harry meets him in *Chamber of Secrets* on a "dying day" when Fawkes bursts into flame and rises as a chick from his own ashes.

Given Fawkes's role in the defeat of the basilisk in *Chamber of Secrets*, Harry's draw with Voldemort in *Goblet of Fire* in the cage of phoenix song and light, and that Dumbledore's adult army in opposition to the Dark Lord is called the Order of the Phoenix, this symbol is central to any interpretation of the books or understanding of their power and popularity. How is the phoenix a symbol of Christ? In the Middle Ages the phoenix, because of its ability to "rise from death," was known as the "resurrection bird." Like the griffin, it was used in heraldic devices and shields to represent the bearer's hope of eternal life in Christ.[15] A sure pointer to this symbolism comes in the climactic battle between Dumbledore and Voldemort in *Order of the Phoenix*. Voldemort has managed to get the drop on his headmaster nemesis and shoots out the death curse, *Avadra Kedavra*. Fawkes the phoenix dives between Dumbledore and certain death, swallows the death curse in his place, explodes into flames, and rises from the dead on the spot. The phoenix here, of course, portrays not only the resurrection of Christ but also his having intervened for us and taken the curse of death upon himself.

The Stag

Lupin and Black explain to Harry in the crucible of the Shrieking Shack that his father, James, was an animagus. Harry discovers later that night what form his father took: a majestic stag with a full rack of antlers. His nickname at school, Prongs, came from these antlers, which are the stag's weapon and defining characteristic.[16] That Harry's Patronus likewise takes the shape of a stag gives this already powerful symbol even more importance.

Narnia fans recall that the Pevensie children in *The Lion, the Witch and the Wardrobe* only return to Earth from their Narnia kingdom because they pursue the White Stag into a thick wood. Lewis points to their search for Christ as the cause of their return, because Christ is to our world what Aslan is to Narnia. The stag can be described as "a beast, the quest of great hunting parties, who was said to grant wishes to his captors. Lewis, as a student of the Middle Ages, would know of the *symbolism of the stag for Christ*"[17] (emphasis added). Maybe you don't see how a big deer can link our world and the Christian creative principle.

It's simple, really. The power of the symbolism comes from the antlers. Just as the phoenix is the "resurrection bird" because it can rise from its own funeral pyre, so the noble stag "came to be thought of as a symbol of regeneration because of the way its antlers are renewed."[18]

The stag's antlers break off and grow back, tying the animal symbolically to the tree of life and the Resurrection. Given this correspondence, it is no accident that when Harry first sees the stag Patronus who saves him from the dementor's kiss—the living, soulless death worse than death—he sees it "as a unicorn."[19] The stag in Harry Potter, like the unicorn, is a symbol for Christ.

The Centaur

Fawkes is great, but my favorite character in literature may be a centaur out of Narnia because of his last words. In *The Last Battle*, the centaur Roonwit—literally "he who knows the ancient languages"[20]—reveals to King Tirian the signs that calamity is about to strike Narnia. The king sends him on a dangerous mission, and Roonwit is shot by the archers of invading Calormenes he was sent to spy on. But he sends this edifying, otherworldly message as he expires: "Remember that all worlds draw to an end and that noble death is a treasure which no one is too poor to buy."[21]

C. S. Lewis, renowned classicist and medieval scholar of Oxford and Cambridge, was certainly familiar with the conventional interpretations and uses of the centaur as symbol. His centaurs in the

Chronicles of Narnia are often of this reveling type, but in Roonwit's case the centaur is heroic and sacrificial in service to the King. In Harry Potter, similarly, we have passionate centaurs and one heroic example, Firenze, who saves Harry from Voldemort in *Sorcerer's Stone*.

The centaur is first and foremost a symbol of man. It has the head and chest of a man and the body of a horse. The head and chest of a man are man's will, thought, and spirit; the horsey bottom is his desires or passions. The centaur is a comic picture of a man's dual nature as angel and beast. When man is right side up, his angelic part tells the horse desires what to do, as a rider directs a horse; when the beast is in control, however, the belly of the horse drags the chest and head where it wants like a runaway pony.[22]

The heroic centaurs Roonwit and Firenze are both symbols of Christ because, as caricatures of men, they are also imaginative "images of God." Through these characters, Lewis and Rowling refer to a tradition that links a man on a passionate beast with heroic, sacrificial, and saving actions: Christ riding into Jerusalem in triumph on a donkey.

The traditional Christian explanation of why Christ rides in triumph into Jerusalem on a donkey rather than a noble steed is that he wanted to show the hosanna-shouting assembly on the sides of the road a three-dimensional icon or symbol of the obedient man. Thus the donkey (certainly a picture of willful, stubborn desire) serves his master, Spirit and God incarnate in cheerful obedience. Roonwit and Firenze give us this scriptural image of the God-man and the rightly ordered soul . . . another symbol of Christ.

The Hippogriff
I confess to initially thinking that Buckbeak the hippogriff was another one of Rowling's mythological innovations—and a hoot.

I had certainly never heard of one. Turns out, it is the creation of a sixteenth-century Italian court poet named Ludovico Ariosto in his *Orlando Furioso*.[23] The original hippogriff, of whom Buckbeak must be a descendant, is a griffin/centaur cross. "Like a griffin, Ariosto's hippogriff has an eagle's head and beak, a lion's front legs, with talons, and richly feathered wings, while the rest of its body is that of a horse. Originally tamed and trained by the magician Atalante, the hippogriff can fly higher and faster than any bird, hurtling back to earth when its rider is ready to land."[24] The hippogriff is "a kind of supercharged Pegasus, a blend of the favourable aspects of the griffin and the winged horse in its character as the 'spiritual mount.'"[25]

Hippo is the Greek word for "horse" (a hippopotamus is a "river-horse"), and *griff* takes us back to the griffin. A *hippogriff*, then, is a combination horse/lion/eagle, or a centaur with a lion/eagle "top." We have already learned how the griffin in Gryffindor is a symbol of Christ as King of heaven and earth. As a griffin/centaur, the hippogriff, too, suggests Christ's divine conquest of the passions, as evidenced by his donkey ride into Jerusalem.

Hagrid describes hippogriffs to his students as "proud," but they are not proud in the sense of conceit or vanity. They are great-souled and aware of their virtue, which the ignoble misunderstand (Hagrid loves them dearly; he knows!). The noble—even supernatural—Buckbeak in *Prisoner of Azkaban* pecks the disrespectful and shameless Malfoy, is persecuted by the godless Ministry, and is almost executed by the Death Eater McNair. He escapes death at the hands of a world that cannot understand him (and that chooses to hate and fear him) to serve as Sirius's salvation. As with the griffin's and centaur's double-natured symbols, Rowling uses the hippogriff as a symbol of Christ, the God-man.

The Philosopher's Stone

The end result of the alchemical Great Work was a stone that produced the Elixir of Life (often called the red lion). This magical object, known as the philosopher's stone, gave its owner immortality (as long as the owner drank the elixir) and infinite wealth. Touching any leaden or base metal object to the stone would make it turn to gold.

Historians of science, religion, and literature agree on very little, in my experience. However, they do agree that the philosopher's stone is a symbol of Christ.[26] There isn't anything else in the world that promises eternal life and golden (that is, incorruptible or spiritual) riches except Christ, so the connection is transparent. The end product or aim of alchemy is life in Christ; English authors and poets of many centuries have used this symbol of Christ, consequently, to dramatize the search for an answer to death and human poverty of spirit. Harry Potter is no exception, as we will see in chapter 11 on *Harry Potter and the Sorcerer's Stone.*

The Red Lion

Narnia fans have told me they see Aslan, Lewis's Christ figure from the Chronicles of Narnia, in the Gryffindor House lion symbol. I think that is a reasonable link, especially in light of the symbolic meaning of Gryffindor and its opposition to the Slytherin serpent. This idea, however, hasn't been "lifted" from Lewis—the lion, and specifically the red lion, has been a symbol of Christ from the first century.

Saint John the Evangelist had no need to explain this usage in the book of Revelation: "Weep not: behold, the Lion of the tribe of Juda, the Root of David, hath prevailed" (Revelation 5:5, KJV). It is a theme of Christian literature and heraldic signs, conse-

quently, throughout the Middle Ages. Lewis draws from this tradition both for Aslan (Persian for "lion") and Aslan's devotees in
Narnia. Remember Peter's shield? "The shield was the color of silver and across it there romped a red lion, as bright as a ripe straw-
berry at the moment when you pick it."[27] The six Harry Potter
books are full of alchemical imagery, and even if Lewis was
unaware of it (the silver and red in Peter's shield makes me doubt
his ignorance), we can assume Rowling knows what the "red lion"
means to an alchemist.[28] The "red lion" is the Elixir of Life coming from the philosopher's stone, a symbol of the blood of Christ
received in Communion. The stone in the first Harry Potter book,
in case we missed this point, is described as "blood red."[29] The red
lion, then, is still another symbolic point of correspondence
between Christ and the world of Harry Potter.

The following chart recaps the eight symbols of Christ we've
examined:

Symbol	Meaning	Therefore
Philosopher's Stone	Transforming lead to gold = Immortality Fount of Elixir of Life = Communion	Christ
Red Lion	Life-giving alchemical elixir; Aslan Revelation 5:5	Christ
Gryffindor = Golden Griffin	Eagle/Lion = Kings of heaven/earth = God/Man = Two natures of Christ	Christ
Unicorn	Biblical references: Numbers, Psalms, Job Christian tapestry & literary tradition	Christ
Phoenix	Resurrection bird; immortal life Medieval literature theme	Christ
Stag	Tradition: "Tree of Life" in antlers Regeneration of antlers = Resurrection	Christ
Centaur	Perfect man in control of passions Christ riding donkey into Jerusalem	Christ
Hippogriff	Eagle/Lion/Horse, Heaven/Earth, God/Man Two natures of Christ	Christ

Does it seem odd that there are so many symbols of Christ? There is a big difference between symbols and allegorical figures. Allegories are stand-ins or story translations of a worldly character, quality, or event into an imaginative figure or story. There can be only one figure representing the other, consequently, or it's difficult to translate; I cannot have two Hitler figures if I'm writing an allegory of the Second World War, or the allegory fails.

Symbols, in contrast, can be stacked up. If I am telling a fantasy story with a Christian message, I can include characters and beasties and events that all point to the various qualities, actions, and promises of Christ. Rowling, depicting Dumbledore's suffering in the cave and in his death on the Astronomy Tower in *Half-Blood Prince,* is writing in story form of Christ's death on the cross at Calvary.[30] If the symbols correspond with these qualities, even if they are not consciously understood as Christ symbols, they open us up to an imaginative experience of those supernatural qualities. A variety of these symbols woven into a story that itself echoes the Great Story will powerfully stir the soul because the heart is made by God to be receptive to this message. Our soul radio is always tuned to the frequency of this message.

The Harry Potter stories, in their formulaic journeys that end every year with love's triumph over death in the presence of a Christ symbol, find their power and popularity in the resonance they create in our heart. We connect with them because they point toward the True Myth that saves us. So much of Harry Potter—the symbols of Harry, Ron, and Hermione; the drama of the soul's faculties in action; the imagery of the many beasts; the windows into Christ's role in the Great Story; and the stories themselves—all foster a Christian perspective by "baptizing the imagination."[31] The gospel has rarely, if ever, been smuggled into the heart and mind of readers so successfully and profoundly.

Now that we have examined the formulas, themes, and symbols of the books, we have only to detour briefly to decipher the secret names many Harry Potter characters have before jumping into the stories themselves.

10
FUN WITH NAMES

*The character names are delightful puzzles
with hidden Christian meanings.*

I confess to enjoying one aspect of Harry Potter's magical world more than all the others: the names of the characters. Rowling has said that she collects names for both their sound and their meaning, and no doubt she has made up a few to suit her purposes.

In this, we can see a tip of the hat to Charles Dickens, whose novels are peppered with names rich and often comic, both in the way they strike the ear and in what they reveal about the so-named person.

As much as I love Dickens, I think the names used in Harry Potter are as good as, and more often than not, better than Dickens's best. Take, for example, the three chasers on the Gryffindor Quidditch team in the first four Potter books: Alicia Spinnet, Katie Bell, and Angelina Johnson.

The Gryffindor team is something of a team of destiny, struggling to win the Quidditch Cup after years of dominance by the Slytherin thugs. The Gryffindors seem to have a higher calling, as suggested by the fact that its chasers' names are church pieces: *spinnet* is an organ, *bell* is what it is, and *angelina* is a decorative angel, wooden or stone, that was commonplace in older English churches. Olive wood, which is the preferred material for church devotional carvings, is reflected in the Gryffindor House's "flying chapel." And who replaces one of the Weasley twins as a Beater in *Order of the Phoenix?* A boy named Kirke, the German word for church![1]

Not *all* the names have two or three layers to them. Some are evidently there just to cue us in to the ethnic diversity you'd expect at a twenty-first-century school in the United Kingdom. Cho Chang, Padma and Parvati Patil, Lee Jordan, Justin Finch-Fletchley, and Seamus Finnegan represent the minority members from the periphery of the old Empire who are rapidly becoming the majority (except for the blue-blooded Finch-Fletchley).

Some names, too, are references to historical magical figures and tips of the hat to Rowling's favorite writers. Minerva McGonagall, Cassandra Vablatsky, and Sibyll Trelawney all have names that point to magical mythology, and Vablatsky is, no doubt, a pointer to the founder of the modern Theosophical Society, Helena Blavatsky.[2]

More fun are the characters from Rowling's favorite writers. Mrs. Norris, Argus Filch's peculiar cat, is no stranger to friends of Jane Austen; Mrs. Norris walks on the stage of *Mansfield Park* with the same aplomb as her feline namesake does at Hogwarts. Robert Louis Stevenson gets a nod or two (Trelawney and Flint are the names of major characters in his adventure novels), the Death Eater Dolokhov echoes Tolstoy, and the Irish representative on campus, Seamus Finnegan, is a probable pointer to the egghead pick for greatest novelist of the twentieth century, James Joyce, and echoes his *Finnegan's Wake.*

My favorite literary reference is to C. S. Lewis. Paul Ford in his

Companion to Narnia explains that the Digory Kirke character in the Narnia novels, the professor who has been to Narnia and who hosts the Pevensie children during the blitz, is a combination of Lewis's tutor, Kirkpatrick, and Lewis himself. Certainly much has been made of the parallel between Lewis and Kirke in their having had sick mothers and providing a safe house for children during the war.

The first Hogwarts champion chosen for the Triwizard Tournament is Hufflepuff House's Cedric Diggory. Harry and Cedric can't be said to be chums (they both have eyes for Cho Chang, for instance), but they help each other through the tournament and in the final trial agree to a tie. Unfortunately, this results in Cedric's death at Voldemort's command.

I believe Cedric Diggory and Digory Kirke are a mirror-image match. No doubt Lewis would have been a Hufflepuff champion— and I believe Dumbledore's command in eulogy to "Remember Cedric Diggory!" is a celebration of the great Christian artist and apologist C. S. Lewis.

Sometimes a character's name tells us what animagus form he or she takes. Rita Skeeter, if not a mosquito, is an insect animagus. The late Sirius Black's first name is the word for the "dog star," and his surname points to his ability to change himself into a big black dog. That Sirius was given to depression and self-pity is also suggested; his name can be pronounced as "Serious Black."

Remus Lupin is not an animagus whose Transfigurations are benign or self-chosen, but his name, too, tells us what he changes into at the full moon. Remus was one of the founders of Rome who was said to have been raised by a wolf, and *lupine* is the English word for "like a wolf." No surprise, then, when Lupin turns out to be a werewolf.

Albus Dumbledore's name may also fit into this category. We were not told what animagus form this former Master of

Transfigurations took, but there were several clues that he was the tawny owl at the opening of *Sorcerer's Stone* and *Prisoner of Azkaban*. However, if his name was the indicator of his animal shape, then he must have been a white or albino bumblebee because this is what *Albus Dumbledore* literally means.

In chapter 4 we discussed the names with alchemical significance. Sirius Black, Albus Dumbledore, and Rubeus Hagrid have names that correspond with the black, white, and red stages of the Great Work. Hermione's first and last names point to her as a budding alchemist; *Hermione* is the feminine form of "Hermes," not only Mercury on Mt. Olympus but also the first great alchemist in Egypt, and *Granger* can mean "farmer." Farming and alchemy are linked because some think that *alchemy* comes from the Egyptian words for "black earth," referring to the floodplains of Egypt that could be tilled successfully.

James and Lily Potter, too, have names with alchemical meaning. Saint James is the traditional patron saint of alchemists, and both Lily and Luna Lovegood have first names that are used as symbols to represent the second, or white, stage of the transformation process.

Why bother studying the meanings of these names? Beyond just the fun of solving a puzzle, I think there are at least two reasons to play the name game: for insights into the character and for a deeper understanding of the story's meaning.

I enjoy playing with the names to see if I can tease out something about what sort of person would carry such a name. Here are a few of my reflections:

- **Severus Snape:** I thought that Snape was a "cutting" personality because his first and last name both seem to be conjugate forms for severing or snipping. However,

I read in the Rev. Francis Bridger's *A Charmed Life* that *snape* is "an English word meaning 'chide' or 'rebuke,'" and hence the whole name means "severe rebuke," an activity for which Snape is well known.[3] Those who believe that Snape is a half vampire, of course, think that the name should be pronounced "sever his nape." But vampires bite the neck; they don't cut it off. Perhaps since so many clues in the books point to a beheading, can we guess what might happen to the Potions Master? The name is a hint![4]

- **Peter Pettigrew:** I have read the strangest interpretations of what Peter's name may mean (many in my Barnes and Noble University classroom in response to my own thoughts). My favorite was from a young woman who understood the name to mean "betrayer—pet who grew." Peter, she explained, was the apostle who betrayed Christ, just like Pettigrew betrayed the Potters. "Pet who grew" she felt was an undeniable allusion to what Scabbers did in the Shrieking Shack in *Prisoner of Azkaban.*

  Neat thinking—but unlikely (although I enjoy "pet who grew"). Judas, after all, betrayed Christ, not Peter. I think it is more likely that with his name Rowling is pointing to Peter's failings in masculine virtue. She has already made him become a rat animagus; the name should suggest something nasty about this coward and turncoat who betrayed his friends to Voldemort.

- **The Weasleys:** Everyone loves the literally poor Weasleys. Fred and George are a riot, Ron is the best friend you could want, Ginny is fun, Arthur and Molly are believable and endearing as the struggling parents of a big family with a small income, Bill and Charlie have played their cameo parts well, and Percy . . . well, every family has its black sheep.

But what's with that last name? The first names are all heroic and larger-than-life—kings, martial saints, and renowned knights all—but "like a weasel"? What's the deal?

And it's not just the name. The Weasleys live at "The Burrow," which is just outside the village of Ottery St. Catchpole. It seems as if all indicators are pointing to their being like weasels. A little reflection, I think, brings out an important point.

Mr. Weasley, who works in the Misuse of Muggle Artifacts Office, is a notorious misuser of Muggle artifacts. As Ron tells Harry in *Chamber of Secrets*, "If he raided *our* house, he'd have to put himself under arrest."[5] Fred, George, Ron, and Ginny have a remarkable ability to think rules are for others—and even pompous Percy thinks that privilege of place means being above the law (note his defenses of Crouch in *Goblet of Fire*). The Weasleys *are* more than a little weaselly, truth be told—and their sensitivity to any use of the word "weasel" reflects this.

More sympathetically, the weasel is one of Rowling's favorite animals. They're team players and are ferociously loyal, according to legend. Of course, the weasel's taste for rats and mice endears them to some, and they are famous for fearlessly taking on animals several times their size.

One source says that weasels are the only animals that can kill the dreaded basilisk, though they die sacrificially in this effort. Because of the link in the popular mind of the basilisk/cockatrice with the devil, the weasels' sacrifice to save others has made them a popular symbol of Christ. A great name for these bold, redheaded fighters![6]

- **Argus Filch:** The squibb caretaker at Hogwarts is named for the watchman in Greek mythology who watches the gates of hell. (That Argus had a thousand eyes is a nice help for a watchman.) *Filch*, which means "to steal," suggests both "filth" and "petty thievery."

So we're left with a contradiction, or at least an unhealthy situation: "a thieving watchman" or "a caretaker with sticky fingers." Filch is neither wizard nor Muggle and is treated disdainfully by everyone except Dumbledore (and Dolores Umbridge, whose sadism he shares).

Filch's name tells us to watch him as a potential turncoat to Lord Voldemort and the Death Eaters. Though they have no love for his kind, they will use the castoffs and neglected members of the magical world for their own ends (as they did Kreacher).

- **Neville Longbottom:** Neville's name points to his "nobody" status. *Neville* breaks down to *ne*, meaning "no" or "not," and *ville*, "villa" or "village," for a sum of "noplace" or "nowhere." *Longbottom* gives us *long*, "big in size or duration in time," and *bottom*, "lowest place," for a composite of either "big buttocks" or "long time at bottom of heap." Every day Neville answers to a name meaning "nowhere-man big-bottom/low-caste." How appropriate that Harry tells Stan Shunpike while hiding on the knight bus that his name is Neville Longbottom.[7] Besides pointing to Harry's shared destiny with Neville, it's a great name for an unassuming alias.

  Neville, however, becomes a man to be dealt with in *Order of the Phoenix*. He works harder than anyone else in D.A. class and more than acquits himself in the battle with the Death Eaters under the Ministry of Magic at book's end. He saves Harry more than once, and if the prophecy was destroyed, it wasn't for lack of heroic sacrifice on Neville's part.

So look for more from Neville than his name would suggest. Both he and Harry, despite Dumbledore's denying it, qualify as potential vanquishers of Voldemort according to the prophecy made before their births. Neville has been "marked" by the destruction of his parents' minds. Harry might have been able to pick up the prophecy glass because of his relationship with Voldemort. Neville or Neville/Harry are still, consequently, possible prophesied Dark Lord vanquishers. Remember that it is Neville's courage in *Sorcerer's Stone* that defeats the Slytherins at book's end; this suggests a foreshadowing of the end in which "the last will be first." Mr. Nowhere-Man may be the hero at series' end, too.

I could go on and on (what do you mean, I have already?). I'd love to tell you about Dolores Umbridge and what "grievous shadow" means as a name for the Hogwarts High Inquisitor. And Irma Pince the librarian? Move that *r* in Irma and you have "I'm a Prince"—and we meet Severus Snape's mother in hiding!

Okay, enough fun for now. Let's get to the names of the major players and see what they tell us about this story and the Great Story.

DUMBLEDORE/VOLDEMORT

Albus Dumbledore, as noted above, has a name that means "white, glorious, resplendent" and "bee." The bee is a traditional symbol for the soul (bees move in clouds that struck many as a visible sign of how the Spirit "bloweth where it listeth" [John 3:8, KJV]). No surprise to find that the champion of all magical creatures, witches, wizards, and Muggles against the madness of the Death Eaters has a name pointing to his sanctity; "resplendent soul" recalls the light of Mt. Tabor (Matthew 17:1-9).

We've already examined Tom Marvolo Riddle. The birth name of the Dark Lord (whose letters can be rearranged to spell "I am Lord Voldemort") tells us his life is about his solving the "riddle" of his "twin" nature (*Thomas* is Aramaic for "twin"). Because he denies his being double-natured—a fallen human yet made in the image of God—he takes on the name Lord Voldemort, which can be interpreted as "willing death," "flight of death," or "flight *from* death." He imagines himself both as an angel of death and as an immortal who has escaped from death.

His exaggerated pride and the denial of both his humanity and access to divinity cause the birth of his vanquisher, who is his doppelgänger ("one in nature, two in essence"). But I'm getting ahead of myself. The names confirm what we learned about Riddle/Voldemort in chapter 5 on doppelgängers.

POTTER/MALFOY

The wicked family in Harry Potter is the Malfoy clan. The father's name is Lucius, and the mother is Narcissa. Their little boy, the darling of Slytherin House, is Draco—the Latin word for "dragon" or "serpent." The serpent is a traditional Christian symbol for the devil, because the evil one takes the form of a snake in the Garden of Eden. C. S. Lewis, in *The Voyage of the Dawn Treader*, depicts a really nasty little boy (much like Draco) named Eustace Scrubb, who turns into a dragon. Lucius, Draco's daddy, is perfectly wicked. He mistreats his servants, patronizes everyone because of his "pure blood" and wealth, and is rather impatient and nasty to his own boy. He gives Riddle's diary to Ginny Weasley, which almost results in more than a few deaths. In *Goblet of Fire* he reveals himself as a Death Eater and a servant of Lord Voldemort, and in *Order of the Phoenix* he is the leader of the bad guys in the battle for the prophecy.

That is no surprise if you look at his name. *Lucius* suggests "Lucifer," which means "light carrier" in Latin. The angel named Lucifer turned on God and became the devil, or Satan ("the deceiver"). Like his son, Lucius Malfoy has a satanic name.

Mom Malfoy's name is not another name for the devil, but it's pretty bad. Narcissus is a young man in Greek mythology who was very aware of his own good looks. He thought so much of himself that he rejected the love of the nymph Echo. He spent so much time admiring his reflection in a pond that some stories say he drowned, and better ones say he became the beautiful narcissus plant. A narcissist, consequently, is anyone of self-importance and ego (usually a self-loving monster). *Narcissa* is not a nice name— and it has enough sibilants in it that you sound like a snake saying it. (In terms of the doppelgänger apposition of so many characters, it is worth noting that the narcissus flower is of the same family as the lily.)

But the worst part of being a Malfoy is that last name. It is French for "bad faith" or "faith in evil." This can mean anything from "untrustworthy" to "Satan worshipper." I might move if the family next door was named "bad faith"! All the Malfoys are branded as black hats by their first and last names.

Let's look at the names for the good guys, by whom I mean the Potters. Harry Potter's late parents were named James and Lily. These have meanings over and above the few mentioned previously, as you've probably guessed—meanings quite different from the Malfoys' names. James, for instance, is the name of Christ's disciple who was also his brother. This brother was the only sibling to recognize Christ as the Messiah; he became (after the Resurrection, Ascension, and Pentecost) the first bishop of Jerusalem and the man in charge at the council recorded in Acts 15.

You may not be familiar with this connection between James

and Christ, but be sure that the English are. Ambassadors from foreign countries to the British government are said to be going to the Court of Saint James; another name for the British royal court contains "Saint James." The name resonates with royalty, and through Saint James and the divine right of kings, with divinity.

Lily was the name of Harry's green-eyed mother. Lilies are magnificent, showy flowers of various colors and usually have a trumpet shape. They are symbolic of spring, though many people associate this flower with death; a white lily is often put in a corpse's hands before the funeral. This is done because the lily, as a symbol of spring, is also the flower of the Annunciation, the Resurrection, and the promise of Christ's return. Corpses are given a lily in hope of their resurrection with Christ at his second coming. Lily, then, like James, is a name with strong ties to Christianity.[8]

Which leaves us with *Harry Potter*. What does Harry's name mean?

Before beginning this discussion, it's best to acknowledge that Harry Potter, because of the worldwide success of this series, is a brand name in millions of people's minds, much like Mickey Mouse, Coca-Cola, or Apple computers. In this Potter-mania environment in which we live, it is difficult to assert that the names mean anything, because to most it has been a long time since the names were restricted to the boy wizard in these books rather than the social phenomenon his name also describes.

Also working against the assignment of any meaning to the name *Harry Potter* is that the name is not at all unusual. Unlike Severus Snape or Millicent Bulstrode, you may actually know a Harry Potter.[9]

Despite these issues, I still think it's silly to believe that the principal player in the series, a series written by an author clearly fascinated with getting names just right on several levels of meaning, would have a meaningless name. Common sense seems to demand the name be picked over pretty closely. Let's take a look.

HARRY POTTER: THE NAME

Harry can literally mean "to harass, annoy, or disturb." Usually someone described as "harried" is run down by too much work and too many distractions. I don't think that's what our Harry's name is meant to imply, even though he does lead an exciting life and, in *Order of the Phoenix*, several times seems on the edge of a breakdown.

Harry is also the familiar form of the names Henry and Harold. More than one Shakespeare play is about Henry IV—when he was the Prince of Wales, during his wild life with Falstaff before becoming king, and his heroic life thereafter. More than a few critics have suggested this is a clue to what our Harry's future has in store. Given the royalty hint in James, this is a real possibility.

As important is that Harold is consonant with the word *herald*. Harry may be the herald of something new and better. Put that thought on the shelf.

As much as I like "herald," I believe that the Cockney and French pronunciations of Harry's name tell us what his first name means. These pronunciations are made without aspirating or breathing through the *h*. Instead of pronouncing the name as if you were saying he were covered with hair, say it as if you were calling him an airhead: "airy." 'Arry with a long *a* suggests the word *heir*.

The heir is the person who stands to get what someone— usually a parent—will leave behind at death. It is usually used to describe someone who will inherit a great deal of money or a position. A prince, for example, is heir to the king's throne. When the king dies, the prince gets the throne and becomes king.

If Harry means "heir-y," then what is our Harry "heir to" or "son of"? Perhaps this is another pointer to Harry's being Heir of Gryffindor. His name, after all, is not just Harry Potter but Harry *James* Potter. Certainly we are told again and again about Harry's likeness to his biological father.

This may very well be the case. A close look at the name *Potter*, though, points to a larger inheritance than just Harry's biological father's wealth and bloodline. For this job you might want to get a Bible concordance.

Looking up *Potter* in the concordance, we find references to its use in the prophets Isaiah, Jeremiah, and Zechariah, the book of Lamentations, Saint Paul's letter to the Romans, and in the book of Revelation.

Because Tupperware wasn't available in biblical times, it shouldn't be surprising to find mention of potters in Scripture. Pots held everything not kept in baskets. But to what are these Bible references alluding when they mention *potter*? Do they mean human potters?

When Bible scholars cite these "potter" passages, they often refer to God's creation of man as recorded by the prophet Moses. "And the Lord God formed man of the dust of the ground, and breathed into his nostrils the breath of life; and man became a living soul" (Genesis 2:7, KJV).

Other Scripture passages refer to human potters. But even then, they point to the potter's craft of shaping a vessel to indicate God's activity in shaping us as creations in his image. Let's look at a couple of these "potter" references to see what I mean.

In Isaiah 64:8, the prophet says, "But now, O Lord, thou art our father; we are the clay, and thou our potter; and we all are the work of thy hand" (KJV).

Jeremiah says, "Then the word of the Lord came to me, saying, O house of Israel, cannot I do with you as this potter? saith the

Lord. Behold, as clay is in the potter's hand, so are ye in mine hand, O house of Israel" (Jeremiah 18:5-6, KJV).

Paul rebukes the stiff-necked Romans by writing, "Nay but, O man, who art thou that repliest against God? Shall the thing formed say to him that formed it, Why hast thou made me thus? Hath not the potter power over the clay, of the same lump to make one vessel unto honour, and another unto dishonour?" (Romans 9:20-21, KJV).

God is thought of as a *potter*, from the beginning of the Bible to the Epistles. Is there any reason to think this biblical usage survives to our times? Yes, there are abundant reasons to believe that.

Today, Orthodox Christians claim that they worship God in the same way the apostles did, keep the same feasts and fasts, and say prayers that have been said by holy men for centuries. During Great Lent, the time of special prayers and fasting to prepare for the celebration of Christ's resurrection (they call it *Pascha* rather than the druid word *Easter*), the Great Canon of Saint Andrew is recited.

These prayers, said around the world by Orthodox Christians, lead people to call on God in repentance for their sins. One of these prayers says, "In molding my life into clay, O Potter, Thou didst put into me flesh and bones, flesh and vitality. But, O my Creator, my Redeemer and Judge, accept me who repent" (Canon of Saint Andrew 1:10). *Potter* is here the equivalent of Creator, Redeemer, and Judge in referring to God.

Remember that J. K. Rowling, besides being a confessed Presbyterian, studied Latin from her earliest years and at the University of Exeter. As is evident in the books' spells, Latin is almost Rowling's second language. With this in mind, it is meaningful to see that the word *potter* is pronounced *exactly as is the Latin word for father (pater)*. This word, like the English word *father*, is used for both biological father and "Father which art in heaven" (Matthew 6:9, KJV). The most famous prayer in the Western church is the "Our Father," which until the Second Vatican Council's liturgical reforms (not implemented until the late sixties) was said by the world's Roman Catholics as the "Pater Noster"—and of course it still is by many millions in private devotions. Harry's last name, deciphered, is both "God" from biblical usage and "Father" from the Latin.

Harry's name, then, taken altogether, means that he is an heir to God the Father (Pater/Potter) or a herald of the same. I rush to say this does not mean Rowling is offering Harry as a symbol of Christ, or as the Antichrist, or even as an allegorical Christ (which is how some people view C. S. Lewis's Aslan). Harry Potter is not the Son of God as Jesus Christ is, but in the manner that you and I are sons of God. Harry is the fallen man seeking to be both image and likeness of God. He is fallen, but he is a seeker (see Matthew 7:7).

Saint Athanasios the Great, a hero and confessor of the early church, said that God became man that man might become God. Athanasios, who stood before the Aryan onslaught for the truth, believed that by means of his incarnation, sinless life, and resurrection from the dead, Christ made it possible for human beings to share in his resurrection and become "little Christs within Christ" (a phrase attributed to Saint John Chrysostom). Man seeking God succeeds in Christ.

That Harry is given a name that means "heir," "herald," or even "son of God" points us to what the saints have taught for two thousand years. We are to love God, not in fear as slaves or in hollow obedience as servants, but as dutiful sons created in his image, who live in joyous expectation of our inheritance—at *our* death, if not before.[10] Harry Potter as "son of God" is not a symbol of Jesus Christ but of humanity pursuing its spiritual perfection in Christ.

Harry Potter is Everyman, hoping to live as God's image *and* likeness, now and in joy for eternity.

The review of the Harry Potter books that we have made so far in these first chapters, looking at the structures, themes, predominant symbolism, even the names of the principal characters, indicates that they are consistent with the Christian worldview and strongly echo its teachings. In the second part of the book, we'll take a quick look at each Harry Potter novel. I doubt, after what you have read so far, that you will be surprised to learn they are profound, edifying Christian morality tales.

II

THE PURIFICATION
OF THE SOUL

Christian keys to Harry Potter
and the Sorcerer's Stone

The first ten chapters of this book include discussions of the elements that run through all the books with an eye toward the Christian meaning of these themes, structures, and symbols. In the next five chapters, we'll look at each book, not, I hope, to repeat what has already been said about love and death and specific Christian symbols, but to reveal the several parts of these books that have "jumped off the page" in terms of Christian meaning.

Much of the first book's meaning is about alchemy. The original title, *Harry Potter and the Philosopher's Stone*, cues us to that. As we'd expect, knowing the alchemical formula, Harry moves through the black stage (the Dursleys, Snape), the white stage (Dumbledore), and the red stage (Rubeus, crisis event). The last is the red-hot crucible scene, in which Harry dies and rises from the dead in the presence of a symbol of Christ (here, the philosopher's stone he pulls from the Mirror of Erised).

In addition to alchemy, there are two other striking parallels with the Christian journey in *Sorcerer's Stone:* the drinking of unicorn blood and the consequences for Quirrell when he tries to kill Harry.

Perhaps the scariest scene in the first book (and certainly the most misunderstood) is the detention in the Forbidden Forest where Harry and Draco see the Dark Lord drinking unicorn blood. "The cloaked figure reached the unicorn, lowered its head over the wound in the animal's side, and began to drink its blood."[1]

Harry is saved by Firenze the centaur, who explains to Harry why someone would drink unicorn's blood:

"Harry Potter, do you know what unicorn blood is used for?"

"No," said Harry, startled by the odd question. "We've only used the horn and tail hair in Potions."

"That is because it is a monstrous thing to slay a unicorn," said Firenze. "Only one who has nothing to lose, and everything to gain, would commit such a crime. The blood of a unicorn will keep you alive, even if you are an inch from death, but at a terrible price. You have slain something pure and defenseless to save yourself, and you will have but a half-life, a cursed life, from the moment the blood touches your lips."[2]

As we saw earlier, the centaur is a symbol of a perfect man and an imaginative icon of Christ riding into Jerusalem. Here, this centaur is talking about another symbol of Christ: the unicorn. That the blood of the unicorn will curse those who drink it unworthily, and that it has life-giving power, echoes Paul's discourse on the unworthy reception of Communion, which is the blood of Christ:

For I have received of the Lord that which also I delivered unto you, That the Lord Jesus the same night in which he was betrayed took bread: And when he had given thanks, he brake it, and said, Take, eat: this is my body, which is broken for you: this do in remembrance of me. After the same manner also he took the cup, when he had supped, saying, This cup is the new testament in my blood: this do ye, as oft as ye drink it, in remembrance of me. For as often as ye eat this bread, and drink this cup, ye do shew the Lord's death till he come. Wherefore whosoever shall eat this bread, and drink this cup of the Lord, unworthily, shall be guilty of the body and blood of the Lord. But let a man examine himself, and so let him eat of that bread, and drink of that cup. For he that eateth and drinketh unworthily, eateth and drinketh damnation to himself, not discerning the Lord's body.
(1 Corinthians 11:23-29, KJV)

Christians have disputed amongst themselves what eating and drinking the body and blood of Christ means, especially in regard to doing it "in remembrance." Men of good will, however, would be hard pressed to feign confusion about what happens to the Christian who does this "unworthily." They're damned, sure and simple.

Now, when Firenze the centaur explains to Harry that anyone who selfishly drinks the life-saving blood of the unicorn is "cursed" from the moment the blood touches his lips, he does everything but read from 1 Corinthians, chapter and verse.

Less explicit but just as important are the smuggled theological points in Harry's journey to the Mirror of Erised and Quirrell's fate in serving the Dark Lord and attacking Harry.

As we've already seen, alchemical work can be described as a salvation journey, using the terms *purification, dissolution,* and *recongealing.* The end result of alchemy is a soul that has turned or "transmuted" from lead to gold, from base desires and concerns for individual advantage to Christlike love and freedom.

Harry Potter and the Sorcerer's Stone is largely an exposition of the alchemical method shown through human character reagents. It is centered on Harry's spiritual purification so that he might be worthy of the Stone at the book's end; this requires his purification, dissolution by contraries, and philosophic congealment.

In chapter 8, we saw that change is a key theme in Harry Potter. In this first book, Harry changes from an orphan in a Muggle home into a wizard hero capable of saving the world from Voldemort's return. This happens in stages as the various character reactants distill the Muggle out of him. His final trials to get the Stone are symbols of his soul's journey to perfection.

Let's look at these trials. They begin with Fluffy, the giant three-headed dog that guards the trapdoor hiding the Stone. Hagrid purchased Fluffy from a "Greek chappie" in a bar— which makes sense, because the dog clearly refers to Cerberus, who played a role in several Greek myths as the monster guarding the gates of hell. Orpheus got past Cerberus by lulling him to sleep with a lyre, and that is Fluffy's weak point as well. Quirrell uses a harp (much like a lyre), and Harry uses Hagrid's gift flute.

Cerberus, the otherworldly canine, is at the gates guarding the gauntlet of trials to the Stone (or spiritual perfection) because the first step in spiritual life and alchemical work is renunciation of the world. This is the first rung on the "ladder of divine ascent," and the most difficult.[3] The power-obsessed Quirrell/Voldemort struggles with the Fluffy obstacle above all others, which is why it takes him so long to enter through the trapdoor.

Renunciation is the better part of purification, and it is not until Harry throws off earthly concerns (the house cup, detentions, being expelled, life itself) that he is able at last to enter the trapdoor. In a heroic scene, he dismisses Ron and

Hermione's concerns about school and family before the prospect of the return of Voldemort and takes the plunge.[4]

The trials the trio goes through to get to the Stone aren't arbitrarily assigned. We saw in chapter 9 how Hermione, Ron, and Harry are actually living symbols of the powers of the soul: Mind, Body, and Spirit (or Mind, Desire, and Heart). This Platonic doctrine of the soul (after its baptism and correction) became the teaching of the church. The trials, though, aren't from Plato but from Aristotle.

Each trial Harry faces in his race to get the Stone, believe it or not, reflects a faculty or kind of soul in the Aristotelian model. The path to the Stone is an obstacle course symbolizing the soul's qualities and powers as presented in Aristotle's *On the Soul* and adapted by medieval theologians. To reach perfection (the philosopher's stone), Harry must necessarily show himself to have surpassed each obstacle within himself.

The Scholastic model, following Aristotle and Aquinas, is that there are three kinds of souls: vegetative, sensitive, and intellective. The powers or faculties closely tied to each kind are: (1) nourishment and reproduction with the vegetative; (2) discrimination and will with sensitivity to data; and (3) the rational and spiritual with the intellective kind.[5] What do Harry, Ron, and Hermione find when they jump through the trapdoor? They descend "miles under the school" into a netherworld crucible where their worthiness will be tested. Then, in sequence from carnal to spiritual, this trio of the soul's powers pass through tests for their purification.

First is the test for the vegetative kind of soul, by means of the vicious plant "devil's snare." Then comes discrimination, or choice.[6] The team has to find the single winged key that fits the locked door at the opposite end of the Chamber, out of hundreds of flying keys. The right "key" here means both "answer unlocking a problem" and "musical note" perceived by the Heart. Desire or Mind cannot hear, find, or catch the right key except in obedience to Heart. Next test, please.

To pass the magical chessboard test, they must become players and win the game. Ron is in charge here, because this is the ultimate test of the willing, or desiring, faculty he embodies. Of course, Ron chooses the passionate, erratic knight and assigns the linear, analytical Hermione the rook (which only moves in straight lines). Harry, the Heart or spiritual center, becomes—what else?— a bishop.

Why is the chess game—what Americans think of as an egghead sport—the test for will and the last or highest test for Ron, our desiring part? Because to win this game, Ron must sacrifice himself. There is no greater challenge for the passionate faculty than to forgo its selfish interest and focus on the greater good. Ron transcends himself in selfless sacrifice, and the test is passed. On to the next test. Don't forget to jump over the troll.

"Pure logic!" Snape has left a word puzzle beside seven bottles of potions that will kill or liberate. This is Hermione's exam, of course, and Mind solves the puzzle without trouble. But this is the end of the road for Hermione; the last test is only for the highest faculty of soul, and she retires, deferring to Harry.

And this test? It's our old friend the Mirror of Erised. Quirrell/Voldemort are standing in front of it, trying to find the Stone, and all Quirrell can see is himself giving it to Voldemort. After the test Dumbledore tells Harry why this is: "You see, only one who wanted to *find* the Stone—find it, but not use it—would be able to get it, otherwise they'd just see themselves making gold or drinking Elixir of Life."[7]

Quirrell/Voldemort is clueless in front of the Mirror, but not Harry. Because of Dumbledore's coaching about the Mirror months before, and his understanding that the happiest man in the world would see only his reflection, Harry knows what he will see—it won't be his family. After the trials of purification he has just passed through, Harry knows he will see himself only wanting the Stone for itself.

> *What I want more than anything else in the world at the moment, he thought, is to find the Stone before Quirrell does. So if I look in the Mirror, I should see myself finding it—which means I'll see where it's hidden! But how can I look without Quirrell realizing what I'm up to?*[28]

The authentic and accomplished alchemist is able to produce the Stone because of his spiritual achievement. It is a *by-product* of that perfection, as are immortality and the riches of transcending the world, rather than the *end* or goal of it. We know Dumbledore and Flamel are of this perfected type because they destroy the Stone at book's end.

Dumbledore has set up the final hurdle to getting the Stone in poetic fashion; the Mirror reflects the spiritual quality of whoever stands before it. To produce the Stone from the Mirror, the seeker must be passionless, which is to say, not desiring any private gain or advantage. One's worthiness to hold or find the Stone is a *reflection* of the quality of one's desires. Quirrell, consumed by Voldemort and his own lust for power, cannot get the Stone—but Harry, of course, sees himself put the Stone in his own pocket.

This is all very interesting, I hear you saying, but what do alchemy, Aristotle, and this Mirror/Stone puzzle have to do with Christianity? Good question. The answer is "quite a bit," although it's not as obvious as the unicorn blood.

Alchemy was not its own religion or spiritual path—it only existed as a discipline within revealed traditions. To Christians, the alchemical process was symbolic of the way to spiritual perfection, and the philosopher's stone, as the end result of this process, was a symbol for Christ.

Having completed a trial by fire and spiritual purification, Harry is able to see and receive this symbol of Christ, because he has no desire to use it for his own advantage but seeks it in loving service to others. Only the pure in heart will see God (Matthew 5:8), and the Mirror reflects the heart's desire.

The purified Harry sees and receives the Stone (Christ), then flees from the two-faced evil of Quirrell/Voldemort—and something fascinating happens. The two-headed monster is unable to touch or have any contact with Harry without burning, quite literally. Dumbledore saves Harry in the end and (after Harry's three-day resurrection) explains what happened:

"But why couldn't Quirrell touch me?"

"Your mother died to save you. If there is one thing Voldemort cannot understand, it is love. He didn't realize that love as powerful as your mother's for you leaves its own mark. Not a scar, no visible sign . . . to have been loved so deeply, even though the person who loved us is gone, will give us some protection forever. It is in your very skin. Quirrell, full of hatred, greed, and ambition, sharing his soul with Voldemort, could not touch you for this reason. It was agony to touch a person marked by something so good." [9]

If there is a single meaning to the Potter books, as we saw in chapter 7 on love and death, it is that love conquers all. And of all loves, sacrificial love is the most important, because it has conquered death. Harry's protection against the assault of the evil one is the love shown years ago by someone who made the greatest sacrifice for him. His bond with that sacrifice and the love it demonstrated permeates his person and repels all evil. Voldemort cannot touch him because of Harry's worthiness to receive the Stone (Christ), and because of the Christlike love and sacrifice that shield him.

Let me take this a step further. Another echo of Christian teaching in the end of Quirrell/Voldemort is in the burning of Quirrell's hands and skin when they make contact with Harry; Quirrell burns and dies in agony. Rowling tells in graphic story form here the traditional Christian doctrine concerning God's judgment and the nature of heaven and hell. One Christian theologian explains it this way:

> God is Truth and Light. God's judgment is nothing else than our coming into contact with truth and light. In the day of the Great Judgment all men will appear naked before this penetrating light of truth. The "books" will be opened. What are these "books"? They are our hearts. Our hearts will be opened by the penetrating light of God, and what is in these hearts will be revealed. If in those hearts there is love for God, those hearts will rejoice seeing God's light. If, on the contrary, there is hatred for God in those hearts, these men will suffer by receiving on their opened hearts this penetrating light of truth which they detested all their life.[10]

Another theologian explains:

> God himself is both reward and punishment. All men have been created to see God unceasingly in his uncreated glory. Whether God will be for each man heaven or hell, reward or punishment, depends on man's response to God's love and on man's transformation from the state of selfish and self-centered love, to God-like love which does not seek its own ends. . . . The primary purpose of Orthodox Christianity, then, is to prepare its members for an experience which every human being will sooner or later have.[11]

Back to Harry and Quirrell. Professor Quirrell is possessed by the evil one. He stands before the judging Mirror, looking at the quality of the desires reflected from his heart. It sees what possesses him: a selfish and self-centered love apart from God. He is unworthy of the Stone/Christ and the ensuing Elixir of Life, so these are kept from him. When he touches someone blanketed by the sacrificial love of a savior (here, of course, Harry's mother) and worthy of having Christ in him, the love of God therein burns Quirrell. His judgment reflects the judgment of hell that rejecters of God will experience.

So what is *Harry Potter and the Sorcerer's Stone* about? Written in the symbolism of alchemy and traditional Christian doctrine, it is an ode to the purification and perfection of the soul in Christ and his saving, sacrificial love. The perfected soul at death will experience the glory and love of God as joy; the soul that has not transcended, that has consumed itself with pursuit of power and love of self apart from God, will experience the same glory as agony and fire.

Let me close here with a story. When I first read this book aloud to my children, my then eleven-year-old daughter Hannah (who had read the book with my permission already) was in the room. I asked her why she thought Quirrell couldn't hold Harry. She explained matter-of-factly that Harry was protected by his mother's love and that love burns people with hard hearts "just like heaven and hell being the same place." I was amazed that she'd made the connection on her own. I guess the world will always underestimate the wisdom and courage of its eleven-year-olds.

12
DANGEROUS BOOKS AND EDIFYING BOOKS

Christian keys to Harry Potter
and the Chamber of Secrets

Rowling remarked at the release of *Goblet of Fire* that it and *Chamber of Secrets* were the hardest stories to write and her favorites among the books. She hasn't told us why, but I have a good guess.

Chamber of Secrets operates on several levels. As in all the books, it tells a rollickin' good yarn while advancing the larger story of Harry and Voldemort. But *Chamber of Secrets* also provides an answer to her Christian critics within its story and is a "book about books" to boot. It couldn't have been easy to write, but I have to agree with her: *Chamber of Secrets* may be the best single volume of the series. It is simultaneously

- A wonderful mystery/adventure story, tightly plotted
- A series of revelations about Riddle and other characters, which move along the larger story line

- A response to critics via a textbook demonstration of the meaning and power of edifying story

As a book about books, *Chamber of Secrets* discusses the quality, value, and dangers of three separate books: Riddle's diary, Lockhart's oeuvre (lifework), and the very Harry Potter book the reader is holding and experiencing. Let's look at each of these books in turn.

Chamber of Secrets turns on Tom Riddle's diary and what happens when it returns to Hogwarts. When Harry and Ron discover the diary in Moaning Myrtle's toilet, Ron warns Harry about the dangerous magic contained in books to keep him from looking at it. Harry, after Ron's hysterical warnings and barely concealed prediction of a fate worse than death, decides he'll have to read it to find out. I don't doubt that this is a bit of advice for the sensible, sober reader: In the matter of a controversial or supposedly dangerous book, you should read it and decide for yourself what it is about.

However, we know we can't dismiss the possibility that books can be dangerous—for Riddle's diary certainly is. Let's lay out what we know about this evil book:

- It is the diary of Tom Riddle (aka Lord Voldemort)
- Delivered by Lucius Malfoy
- In a Transfiguration textbook
- To Ginny Weasley.

Lucius Malfoy's intentions in planting the book in Ginny Weasley's textbook are not, as one might think, to restore Lord Voldemort. Malfoy could have done that on his own, in Quirrell fashion, with any stooge. Dumbledore tells us that the book planting was a "clever plan" to undermine Arthur Weasley's standing among wizards and to destroy the sponsors of the Muggle Protection Act.[1]

Mr. Malfoy is understandably nervous about this act and the consequent raids to round up "dangerous toys" from dark wizards. Draco Malfoy also suggests that his father was trying to remove the "Muggle-loving" Dumbledore from Hogwarts—which he succeeded in doing, at least for a while.

We can discern an important point about the effects of authentically dangerous books through the example of Riddle's diary:

- The innocent (Ginny can be read as "Virginia" or "virgin," though Rowling revealed after *Phoenix* was published that Ginny's given name is "Ginevra")
- Are transfigured (the diary is placed in the Transfiguration textbook)
- Into the wicked (the possessed Ginny is the one who opens the Chamber and releases the basilisk)
- By the author of a book of dark magic (Riddle/Voldemort is the bad guy)
- That is hidden inside their textbooks and pretending to be what it is not.

The effect of the book on Ginny is that she turns into a rooster-murdering, basilisk-releasing servant of Riddle. She thinks she is losing her mind—and she is right. Her mind is now Voldemort's; in this is the death of her innocence and purity. The effect of the book on Harry, too, is remarkable. After his time inside the memory of Tom Riddle, he more than half-believes that Hagrid is the Heir of Slytherin. It is a pretty powerful drug or Confundus Charm—or evil magic—that could make Harry suspect his friend, the Dumbledore-adoring gamekeeper.

This isn't really a warning to beware of the sneaky diaries of dark wizards. *It's a warning about the dangers hiding in children's textbooks.*

In this, Rowling follows C. S. Lewis's discussion of just this problem in *The Abolition of Man*. The lead essay, "Men without Chests," exposes the harm done by the insidious and sentiment-destroying "moral philosophy" of textbook writers.

Lewis felt strongly that the hidden "dark wisdom" in our children's schoolbooks is what is transforming them from something human into people who are somehow less than human. Because they grew up "having read the wrong sort of books" (as with Eustace Scrubb in *The Voyage of the Dawn Treader* and Mark Studdock in *That Hideous Strength*), they are incapable of the sentiments and emotions that buttress and create moral excellences such as courage. We can see this real danger of the vacant naturalism and godlessness characteristic of textbooks through the mind of Tom Riddle hidden in Ginny's Transfiguration schoolbook.

I also think this is part of Rowling's intended response to the objections to magic in her books. We have already read Lewis's response to his own Christian critics: Magic, he explained, can be a counterspell, and magic in edifying fiction is just that—a counterspell to the enchantment of modernity.

Let's move on to the most comic figure in the Potter series, Gilderoy Lockhart, and take a look at his books. Gilderoy Lockhart sure has written a bunch of books; he is the author of books ranging from how to deal with household pets, his (ahem) adventures around the word, and his favorite subject: himself. Here is what we know is true about each of these books:

- Their only purpose is to generate money and fame for Gilderoy.
- The adventure stories are all the accomplishments of other magical persons.
- Women (that is, witches) love them; wizards do not.

Beyond his being "Order of Merlin, Third Class, Honorary Member of the Dark Force Defense League, and five-time winner of *Witch Weekly*'s Most-Charming-Smile Award" (which he "won't talk about," but manages to mention four times in *Chamber of Secrets*), what we learn about Gilderoy himself is:

- He is despised by the teachers as an empty-headed braggart.
- He is adored by the girl students, but he sickens the boys.
- He lives for publicity, large photos of himself, and other people's admiration.
- He favors effeminate colors in robes (jade, lilac, midnight blue, etc.).
- He has one good trick (the Memory Charm).
- He is a coward ("Order of Scaredy Cat, First Class").

His cowardice is revealed in spades when Ginny Weasley is taken by Riddle into the Chamber of Secrets and the teachers tell Lockhart he has "free rein at last" to slay the monster. When Harry and Ron go to him to explain where they think the Chamber is, he tells them this sort of work wasn't in the job description. He reveals that he has done none of the heroic deeds recounted in his books—and tries to work a Memory Charm on the boys to protect his secret.

Harry and Ron disarm him, then force him to join in their pursuit of the Chamber. When he grabs Ron's broken wand while miles under the school, he causes a cave-in by trying another Memory Charm (the wand explodes). The backfiring charm "obliviates" his memory, which compels Dumbledore to say later, "Impaled upon your own sword, Gilderoy!" Most everyone cheers, professors and students alike, when it is announced at the Leaving Feast that Professor Lockhart "would be unable to return next year, owing to the fact that he needed to go away and get his memory back"

(*Chamber of Secrets*, chapter 18). In books promoting the virtues of bravery, selflessness, and loyalty, you're not supposed to like Gilderoy. We can laugh at him, but we're clearly not supposed to think of him as a role model. Gilderoy is a cartoon figure of everything self-important, self-promoting, superficial, effeminate, and emasculating—everything the Harry Potter books hope to overcome and replace with heroic, masculine virtues.

Even if we never met him, his name alone would tell us we weren't supposed to like him. *Gilderoy Lockhart* breaks down to *gilded*, or "given a deceptively attractive appearance," *roi*, which is French for "king," *lock*, "shut tight," *hart*, "heart." His name tells us he is a false, "pretty boy" prince with a closed heart, which is to say a "hard heart" that is spiritually dead. What more do we need to know?

The fact that his only magic (his "sword") is the Memory Charm reveals the real value of Gilderoy's books. They are lies, written only for the promotion of their author and, one has to guess, "not for guys." Their strength is that they help us forget; they're an escape wherein we can forget what we are about—and what the author really is about too.

I have to believe that Rowling hates Gilderoy's kind of fiction; it's everything her fiction is not. In this second "book within the book," I think she offers this character to her critics as a foil for her own work. Children's literature that does not come from true belief or genuine love and concern for young readers demeans them and distracts them from spiritual combat-readiness. There are no "stock responses" in Gilderoy's books, no right alignment of soul, and certainly no baptism of the imagination in Christian doctrines and symbols. Rather than Christ, the true king, all we find in Lockhart's books is himself: Gilderoy, the "false king."

The point of looking at Gilderoy and his books is to realize that this kind of book is as corrosive to right spiritual formation as the moral relativism and other poisons hiding in textbooks. Godless fiction is slow poison to the soul.[2]

But enough about Gilderoy. On to the third "book" inside *Chamber of Secrets*, which is the story line of *Chamber of Secrets* itself. In contrast with the Lockhart genre and Riddle's diary, the Harry Potter books don't demean or diminish readers by indoctrinating them with worldly philosophies. Here is a book to shape the hearts and minds in a different and much better mold!

This book ends with an answer for the Christian critics: The best books for children are the ones that model for them a heroic life in battle with the evil one, dependent on the graces only available in Christ. That "best book" model is evident in the battle scene at the end of *Chamber of Secrets,* a Christian morality play for anyone with "eyes to see." I believe that the finish to *Chamber of Secrets* is the most transparent Christian allegory of salvation history since Lewis's *The Lion, the Witch and the Wardrobe.* Let's look at it in detail:

- Harry, our Everyman, enters the Chamber of Secrets to find and rescue Ginny Weasley. He finds her unconscious and cannot revive her. He meets Tom Riddle. Because he thinks Riddle is a friend, Harry asks for his help in restoring Ginny. No deal.
- He learns then that Tom Riddle is anything but his friend; Riddle is instead the young Lord Voldemort, Satan's stand-in throughout the Harry Potter books. Far from helping him revive Ginny, Riddle has been the cause of her near death. Harry boldly confesses to Riddle's face his loyalty to Albus Dumbledore and his belief that Dumbledore's power is greater than Lord Voldemort's.
- The Chamber is filled with phoenix song at this confession, heralding the arrival of Fawkes (Dumbledore's phoenix),

who brings Harry the Sorting Hat of Godric Gryffindor. The Dark Lord laughs at what Dumbledore sends his defender and offers to teach Harry a little lesson: Let's match the powers of Lord Voldemort, Heir of Salazar Slytherin, against famous Harry Potter and the best weapons Dumbledore can give him. He releases the giant basilisk from his reservoir, and the battle is joined.

- The look of the basilisk is death, so Harry runs from it with eyes closed. Fawkes the phoenix attacks the charging basilisk and punctures its deadly eyes. Harry cries for help to "someone—anyone" as the phoenix and the blind basilisk continue to battle, and he is given the Sorting Hat by a sweep of the basilisk's tail.

- Harry throws himself to the ground, rams the hat over his head, and begs for help again. A gleaming silver sword comes through the hat.

- Evil Tom Riddle directs the blind basilisk at this point to leave the phoenix and attack the boy. When it lunges for him, Harry drives the sword "to the hilt into the roof of the serpent's mouth"—but one poisonous fang enters Harry's arm as the basilisk falls to its death (*Chamber of Secrets*, chapter 17). Harry, mortally wounded, falls beside it. The phoenix weeps into Harry's wound as Riddle laughs at Harry's death.

- Too late, Riddle remembers the healing powers of phoenix tears and chases away the phoenix. He then confronts the prostrate boy and raises Harry's wand to murder him. The phoenix gives Harry the diary, and Harry drives the splintered basilisk fang into it. Riddle dies and disappears; red ink pours from the diary. Ginny revives, and they escape by holding the tail feathers of the phoenix, who flies from the cavern miles beneath Hogwarts to safety and freedom above. Harry celebrates with Dumbledore.

Now let's translate this morality play and allegory. First, we need to know the cast of characters and places and what reality each represents:

- Harry is Everyman
- Ginny is virgin innocence, purity
- Riddle/Voldemort is Satan, the deceiver
- The basilisk is sin
- Dumbledore is God the Father
- Fawkes the phoenix is Christ
- Phoenix song is the Holy Spirit
- Gryffindor's sword is the sword of the Spirit (Ephesians 6:17)
- The Chamber is the world
- Hogwarts is heaven

The action of this salvation drama, then, goes like this:

Man, alone and afraid in the world, loses his innocence. He tries to regain it but is prevented by Satan, who feeds on his fallen, lost innocence. Man confesses and calls on God the Father while facing Satan, and is graced immediately by the Holy Spirit and the protective presence of Christ.

Satan confronts man with the greatness of his sins, but Christ battles on man's side for man's salvation from his sins. God sends man the sword of the Spirit, which he uses to slay his Christ-weakened enemy. His sins are absolved, but the weight of them still means man's death. Satan rejoices.

But the voluntary suffering of Christ heals man! Man rises from the dead, and with Christ's help, man destroys Satan. Man's innocence is restored,

and he leaves the world for heaven by means of the Ascension of Christ.
Man, risen with Christ, lives with God the Father in joyful thanksgiving.

I can imagine where different types of Christians could disagree with this thumbnail sketch of Everyman's salvation drama, in terms of emphasis and specific doctrines. However, we can all understand the basic structure of the story and admire the artistry of the allegory. Using only traditional symbols, from the Ancient of Days figure as God the Father to the satanic serpent versus the Christlike phoenix (the "resurrection bird"), the drama takes us from the fall to eternal life without a hitch. There's nothing philosophical or esoteric here. (Can you say, "no alchemy"?)

This is why I believe that these books are Christian and in bold opposition to the spiritually dangerous books our children are often given. *Chamber of Secrets* is an unequaled example in the genre that provides an engaging, enlightening, and edifying reading experience for children—as well as a powerful rebuke and wake-up call to Christian critics.

What is *Chamber of Secrets* about? These stories are edifying fiction, written in such a way that they prepare children for Christian spiritual life and combat with evil. Talk about baptizing the imagination with Christian symbols and doctrine!

It's clear from this book that our real enemy is not the magic of Harry Potter, but both the dark magic hidden in our children's textbooks and the "good children's books" written by atheists and the worldly-minded.

Chamber of Secrets is a tour de force operating on at least three levels of meaning simultaneously. I can understand Rowling's struggle in writing it, and I agree with her that it is the best single volume of the series. As a nod to its movie adaptation, I give *Chamber of Secrets* five stars and two thumbs up.

13

DESPAIR AND DELIVERY

Christian keys to Harry Potter
and the Prisoner of Azkaban

Prisoner of Azkaban is a much different book from *Chamber of Secrets.*
In fact, though I have learned that *Prisoner* is far and away the "best
book" according to many Harry Potter fans, many others do not
care for it at all. Please note that the books in the series alternate in
their emphasis and mood. The first, third, and fifth books are relatively "interior" or psychological novels, and the second and fourth
books are "exterior" or social novels. My unprofessional surveys
among serious readers and fans of the books confirm this in that
folks who describe themselves as extroverts prefer Chamber of
Secrets and Goblet of Fire, and self-proclaimed introverts like Prisoner of Azkaban and Order of the Phoenix.

Prisoner of Azkaban is really a book about escapes and revealed
secrets. Who escapes? Who is revealed?

- *Sirius Black* escapes from Azkaban and is revealed to be, not
  the murderer of Harry's parents and servant of Lord

Voldemort (as everyone assumes), but Harry's long-suffering protector and authentic godfather.

- *Buckbeak the hippogriff* escapes execution and is revealed to be, not the dangerous bird the Ministry thinks he is, but the means of Sirius's salvation.
- *Peter Pettigrew*, we learn, escaped Sirius and a death sentence years ago (by feigning his own murder at Black's hands), and he is revealed to be the real Judas. He is a secret-keeper, servant, and spy for Voldemort—as well as the betrayer of James and Lily Potter.
- *Pettigrew* also escapes execution in the present (because of Harry's mercy) along with capture, and is revealed to be an animagus—a rat literally and figuratively.
- *Remus Lupin's* werewolf status is revealed at last, but he "escapes" from his own mistaken beliefs both about his friends Black and Pettigrew and about the limits of Dumbledore's ability to understand and forgive.

The most important escapes, changes, and revelations in *Prisoner of Azkaban*, though, revolve around Harry Potter himself.

- He escapes from Privet Drive and the badgering of Aunt Marge at the beginning of the book, revealing himself to be an angry young man with a host of unresolved issues about his parents and his own identity.
- He escapes from these passions via dissolution of his confusion (and revelation of his past) in the alchemical crucible of the Shrieking Shack, revealing himself by his protection of Pettigrew to be the merciful son of his father.
- He escapes his fears and depression that crystallize in the presence of the dementors, revealing himself by his conjuring

of the Patronus at book's end and by his defeat of the dementor host to be an advanced magician of no little power.

We've already discussed the first two of these escapes and revelations at some length. But Harry's battle to overcome the dementors is the larger part of the plot in *Prisoner of Azkaban*, so it warrants a closer interpretation.

It's important to remember that the dementors are incarnations of depression and despair. Their name reflects this meaning: besides being a demonlike prefix, *de* is Latin for "from" or "out of," while *ment* comes from the Latin word *mens* meaning "mind." The dementors are literally the demonic "drive-you-out-of-your-mind-ers." Lupin gives us some details about these guardians of Azkaban:

> *Dementors are among the foulest creatures that walk this earth. They infest the darkest, filthiest places, they glory in decay and despair, they drain peace, hope, and happiness out of the air around them. Even Muggles feel their presence, though they can't see them. Get too near a dementor and every good feeling, every happy memory will be sucked out of you. If it can, the dementor will feed on you long enough to reduce you to something like itself . . . soulless and evil. You'll be left with nothing but the worst experiences of your life.*[1]

Dementors, then, crush their victims' humanity by feeding on their hope, happiness, and desire to survive. Lupin reports that "they don't need walls and water to keep the [Azkaban island] prisoners in, not when they're all trapped inside their own heads, incapable of a single cheerful thought. Most of them go mad within weeks." But they have a "last and worst weapon . . . the dementor's kiss" by which they "suck out [the victim's] soul." So what? Well, if it happens to you, Lupin explains, "There's no chance at all of recovery. You'll just—exist. As an empty shell. And your soul is gone forever . . . lost."[2]

The kiss is a poetic expression of the human "consolation" found in despair: a living death, worse than physical death—soulless existence. The dementor's effect on Harry even without this kiss is remarkable enough. Just being near one, Harry experiences the live replay of his parents' murders by Lord Voldemort over his crib. Needless to say, this knocks him out and off his feet—and at the climax of a Quidditch match, off his broomstick. The fall nearly kills him, and Gryffindor loses the match.

This won't do. Harry needs a defense against these dementors and goes to the Defense Against the Dark Arts teacher, Remus Lupin. Though Lupin protests that he is not "an expert at fighting dementors . . . quite the contrary,"[3] he agrees to give Harry tutorials in how to dispel a dementor.

In *Prisoner of Azkaban*, Lupin acts as Harry's tutor and de facto Jungian analyst. He is not only coaching Harry in dementor defense, but in his repeated exposure to his parents' dramatic demise, Harry is also overcoming this trauma. This is an echo of Dumbledore's psychological mentoring in *Sorcerer's Stone*, when he taught Harry that it wouldn't do to stand before the Mirror of Erised and long for his dead parents. Harry relearns this critical lesson with Lupin. After one especially traumatic session, Harry reflects:

> *He felt drained and strangely empty, even though he was so full of chocolate. Terrible though it was to hear his parents' last moments replayed inside his head, these were the only times Harry had heard their voices since he was a very small child. But he'd never be able to produce a proper Patronus if he half wanted to hear his parents again . . .*

"They're dead," he told himself sternly. "They're dead and listening to echoes of them won't bring them back. You'd better get a grip on yourself if you want that Quidditch Cup."[4]

Chocolate, the ultimate comfort food, helps speed recovery from exposure to a dementor, but defense from these soul-sucking nasties involves what Lupin and Hermione both classify as extremely advanced magic. What Lupin tries to teach Harry is how to conjure a *Patronus* using the Patronus Charm.

This is no easy feat, and Lupin is pained by the experience as well. When Harry says he heard his father speaking, Lupin almost loses it. No doubt the analyst is experiencing some catharsis of the unresolved issues surrounding James Potter's death, namely, Lupin's still being Black's secret keeper. He almost bites Harry's head off when he is asked in all innocence if he knew Sirius Black.

The Patronus Charm requires the wizard to say the words *"Expecto Patronum"* and to concentrate as hard as possible on a happy memory to fill the heart with joy. At first, Harry is only able to conjure a thin, wispy Patronus when he practices with the Boggart. The problem is he "half wants" to hear his parents even in their death throes. After he gives himself a stern talking-to, he finds he can do it. He conjures a magnificent Patronus while chasing the Snitch at his next Quidditch match and dispels the dementor impersonators from Slytherin.

However, Harry struggles in later attempts to conjure the Patronus, and is only able to do it in the presence of the real thing after his remarkable experience in the Shrieking Shack. A closer look at the words of the charm reveals why—and reveals the larger meaning of *Prisoner of Azkaban* as well.

David Colbert has written a charming companion book for the Harry Potter books called *The Magical Worlds of Harry Potter*. It's a hoot! But in one section called "Latin for Wizards," there's a mistake. Mr. Colbert's Latin is probably in better shape than my own, but he blows the translation of the Patronus Charm. He says *Expecto Patronum* comes "from *expecto*, to throw out; and Patronus, guardian."[5] It makes sense as a charm—"I throw forth a guardian"—but it's not what the Latin says.

Expecto is an ellision of *ek* or *e* ("out from, out for") and *specto* ("look, watch"). *Expecto*, consequently, doesn't mean "to throw out" (that would have been *expello*—as in "I punched the teacher so they expello-ed me from school"). What it does mean is "to look out for, await, long for expectantly." In the Latin version of the Apostles' Creed, the "await, look for" conclusion ("*I look for* the resurrection of the dead and the life of the world to come") begins with the word *expecto*.

Patronus can mean "guardian." But in the context of *Prisoner of Azkaban*, it's good to realize the word comes from the root *pater*, which, as we learned in the discussion of Harry's name in chapter 10, means "father." *Patronus* means "little father" or "second father," which is obvious in the English word that is derived from it: "patron," the person—like Dad—who pays the bills. The word can be used as "godfather" (especially as in the movie with Marlon Brando), "guardian," or "deliverer" (as in "from danger"). In this last sense, "savior" is not a bad or infrequent translation.

Expecto Patronum, consequently, can be interpreted a couple of ways. Because Harry's Patronus comes in the shape of his dad as animagus, you could say it means "I look for the figure of my father."

The way Rowling uses this phrase, however, echoes its use from the Apostles' Creed—"I long for my savior and deliverer." The charm is said in joyful expectation and in faith that deliverance is coming. I have three reasons for thinking this explicitly Christian meaning is the correct interpretation:

I. Lupin isn't very good at this charm. His haunting problem is not his trouble with lunar cycles, but his lack of faith in Dumbledore's love. Dumbledore has been his "second father" and "patron," but Lupin cannot sincerely say *"Expecto Patronum"* with joy and faith because he doesn't trust that Dumbledore would love him if he were to know the truth about him.

2. Harry's Patronus takes the shape of a stag that shines "as bright as a unicorn."[6] Both the stag and the unicorn are traditional symbols of Christ.

3. Harry is able to conjure his Patronus only after the Shrieking Shack experience and after seeing what he thinks is the ghost of his father conjuring a Patronus to save him from the dementor's kiss.

What is it about these experiences that creates the breakthrough for Harry? The Shrieking Shack is an alchemical crucible with character catalysts for Harry's purification, dissolution, and perfection (as in *Sorcerer's Stone*). At the side of the lake, he realizes his identity with his father, on earth as in heaven. That may seem like a reach, so let's walk through it.

In the Shrieking Shack, Harry is surrounded by the alchemical catalysts and colors we learned in chapter 4 and reviewed in the discussion of *Sorcerer's Stone*. Ron is still "red," passionate sulfur; Hermione is still "mercury" or "quicksilver." The black and white elements, however, are different (though Snape makes an appearance when Sirius is revealed to be not so "black"). Sirius Black, of course, takes the "black" part of being unclean: "guilt, original sin, hidden forces." As Dumbledore did with the Mirror in *Sorcerer's Stone*, Lupin this time performs the "white" initial or minor work, clearing away Harry's paralyzing longing for his parents. He has "flecks of gray" in his brown hair; my mental picture of a werewolf (unconfirmed by the text) is of a silver-gray, giant wolf. Close enough to "white."

Under these contrary influences, Harry's anger, misconceptions, and passion dissolve. He learns the identities of Moony, Wormtail, Padfoot, and Prongs, along with the remarkable story of betrayal and escape surrounding the Fidelius Charm that protected Harry's family. He is transformed by these revelations, so he is no longer the out-of-control, angry boy who blew up Maggie Thatcher—I mean, Aunt Marge—on Privet Drive for carelessly insulting his parents. Harry has become a young man capable of forgiving both Black for making Pettigrew the Potters' secret-keeper and Pettigrew for betraying his family to Voldemort.

This last act is one of superhuman mercy, which no one else in the Shack is capable of. The "gold" purified soul does this in imitation of his father. As Harry says, "I'm not doing this [preventing your execution] for you [Pettigrew]. I'm doing it because—I don't reckon my dad would've wanted them to become killers—just for you."[7] This humility, compassion, and mercy is evidence that he has indeed achieved a degree of spiritual perfection; his will and his father's will are one and the same, just as we see in John 17:21 and Matthew 6:10; 26:39.

But Harry is just beginning to realize the connection between himself and his father. They leave the shack, and Lupin transforms into a werewolf in the light of the full moon. Black, too, converts to his animal form to protect everyone from the werewolf, and in the confusion Wormtail escapes. The children hear Black screaming and run to his aid at the side of the lake. Dementors! Harry struggles to conjure a Patronus but fails. He is saved from the dementor's kiss, however, by a spectacular unicornlike Patronus, conjured from across the water by a figure he thinks is his father.

Dumbledore sends Harry and Hermione back in time to rescue

Buckbeak and Black. On this trip, Harry cannot help himself; he has to see if it was his father who saved him. He realizes at last he had not seen his father conjuring the Patronus—he had seen himself. He conjures the spectacular stag Patronus, the image of his father as Prongs (and Christ) that saves Hermione, Sirius, and himself from the dementors. Hermione is stunned that Harry is capable of this sort of advanced magic:

> *"Harry, I can't believe it. . . . You conjured up a Patronus that drove away all those dementors! That's very, very advanced magic. . . ."*

> *"I knew I could do it this time," said Harry, "because I'd already done it. . . . Does that make sense?"*[8]

It makes sense, Harry, but perhaps only if you look at this as a Christian who is familiar with the Gospel according to John.

John's Gospel tells us that the Son's relationship with the Father, and ours to the Father through the Son and his Spirit, are the essential relationships of Christian salvation. That Harry's father appears in the form of a Christ symbol (the stag), and that Harry's deliverance (as son) comes at his realization that he is his father (in appearance and will), are poetic expressions of the essential union of Father and Son for our salvation.

In *Prisoner of Azkaban*, Harry at last comprehends his likeness with his father. By this knowledge he is able to summon a Christ figure as his salvation, in hopeful, almost certain, and joyous expectation of deliverance. He yells "EXPECTO PATRONUM" without having to think a happy thought because his expectation itself is one pure, happy thought.

Sirius Black tells Harry in his last words before flying away from Hogwarts on the wings of a happy hippogriff: "You are—truly your father's son, Harry."[9] Dumbledore tells him during their end-of-book consultation, "I expect you'll tire of hearing it, but you do look *extraordinarily* like James." Harry at the end of *Prisoner of Azkaban* has realized his identity with his father.

THE LESSONS OF AZKABAN

I said at the beginning of this chapter that *Prisoner of Azkaban* isn't an easy book. It is a difficult read, and because of its subject matter, many people have told me they find it depressing—which I think is an understandable reaction. *Prisoner of Azkaban* is about how to combat the demons of the modern world: the depression and despair consequent to lack of faith.

Harry Potter's answer for this problem, though, is anything but depressing. Implicitly, and almost explicitly at times, we see that the answer is our ability to call on Christ in faith. We need to escape our ego attachments and identify instead with our heavenly Father as his children in the Spirit. Following Harry's path, we can find these steps for success in combating despair:

1. **Understand yourself as a child of God in need of patronage and a Savior.** Harry is a troubled young man when he arrives at Hogwarts this year. He enters counseling for tutorial help in understanding his problems. His enlightened counselor steers him toward the advanced magic of selfless and joyous expectation of a deliverer.

2. **Understand that without humility, there can be no grace.** Harry is not equal to this magic until his ego concerns have been purified and dissolved. Only when his family history is clear to him is he capable of the humility necessary to forgive and have mercy. It is a formula that goes back to the church fathers— "No humility, no grace"—that explains Harry's new abilities to see and act after the Shrieking Shack.

3. **In humility and joy, cry out in faithful expectation.** Consequent to his forgiveness and mercy in the Shack (in imitation of his father), Harry is able to see his likeness with his father and to cry out in confident (literally "with faith") expectation of his savior. This achievement is the cure for depression and despair.

4. **Look for the stag (Son of God) to expel despair.** Harry is saved by the stag Patronus that he conjures, and Sirius is saved by the hippogriff Harry and Hermione ride to his tower window. In Christ, we too are delivered from death and from the shadows cast by death in this life: depression and soulless despair.

This may not be as simple a Christian morality play as the one acted out in *Chamber of Secrets*. But it reflects the edifying themes, Christian symbolism, and doctrine that we have seen in all the Potter books. That *Prisoner of Azkaban*, despite its complexity and profundity, did not derail or even slow the Potter-mania juggernaut, speaks to both the hunger for this message and the art with which Rowling delivers it. Although I prefer *Chamber of Secrets* to all the other Harry Potter books, it is *Prisoner of Azkaban* that I reread most often. As a son, man, and daddy, its Christian meaning is especially helpful to me.

Muggles, we read in Harry Potter, cannot see dementors, but they can feel them. Certainly I have felt frightened and alone, Muggle that I am, and my only escape from such fears and isolation is faith in Christ. Harry Potter, and especially the *Prisoner of Azkaban* installment of his annual adventures, is support and encouragement in the faith and in battling the demons of our culture and times.

14

GIRDED WITH VIRTUE

Christian keys to Harry Potter
and the Goblet of Fire

As we've already discussed, the Harry Potter books alternate in emphasis and focus. *Sorcerer's Stone, Prisoner of Azkaban,* and *Order of the Phoenix*—the first, third, and fifth novels—are psychological or inward experiences for Harry. *Chamber of Secrets* and *Goblet of Fire,* in contrast—the second and fourth novels—are less about what Harry learns about himself (his interior life) than what he learns about his world (his exterior life). This alternating of emphasis conforms to the principle of alchemy in which contraction follows expansion (and vice versa) as night follows day and odd numbers follow even.

Goblet of Fire is a big book (certainly the longest single book I had read out loud to my children—until *Phoenix* was published!), and it doesn't lack for events and meaning. Here's a quick summary:

- There are important changes in Harry from the beginning to the end of *Goblet of Fire.* He moves from being a spectator at the World Cup to a school champion to shouldering a grown wizard's burden against the Dark Lord. He matures from a teenager concerned about the opinions of others to a young man of integrity and self-confidence.

- There is an expansion of the story line and focus from Hogwarts and Harry's internal and schoolyard struggles to the world stage and the social drama of good versus evil. Rowling skewers more than a few sacred cows in her satirical portraits of everything authoritative and institutional, from the courts and prisons to schools, the media, government, and sports.

- There is a continuation of the alchemy theme of purification and perfection by trial, both in the crucible of the phoenix song cage with Voldemort and in the four tasks of the Triwizard Tournament. These tasks echo the steps of purification before Harry gets to the Mirror in *Sorcerer's Stone*. The Tournament tasks are keyed to the four elements of alchemy: air, earth, fire, and water. Each suggests classical or medieval tournament sport:

Air: fighting dragons (reference to knights' warfare)
Water: rescuing hostages (again, knights' work)
Earth: finding the center of a maze despite obstacles (Theseus's hero journey)
Fire: combat of the champion with the evil one in a grave-yard (morality play)

As we mentioned in chapter 4's discussion of alchemy, the sequence of *Goblet of Fire*'s Triwizard tasks (dragon to egg to bath to submersion to maze to graveyard), follow the images used to describe the alchemical Great Work. As in *Sorcerer's Stone*, Harry is being prepared for his confrontation with Voldemort at book's end by the obstacles and tasks he must overcome to get there.

In this book, we can see that sport and combat are a metaphor for the spiritual life. Harry and Hermione admire Viktor Krum's decision to grab the Golden Snitch in the World Cup Final—though it meant his team would lose—because it reflected Krum's doing the right thing even if it meant losing. Honor, bravery, sacrifice—this is what we learn in sports, if our focus isn't only on winning and losing. We see it again and again in Harry's choices at the Triwizard Tournament:

- Task 1: Harry clues in Cedric that it's about dragons
- Task 2: Harry saves more than just his hostage
- Task 3: Harry saves Cedric twice in the maze

It has to be noted here that Harry is an *unwilling* champion who *never* prepares properly for his event except in an ad hoc mad frenzy in the days immediately before the event—and that it is always the intervention of outside forces or information that get him through. In the end, Harry has to be ordered by Cedric to share the victory with him. Winning is obviously not the only thing to Harry Potter. In fact, in the Triwizard Tournament, it is barely *anything* to him.

I would go so far as to say that Harry's indifference and his consequent charity and nobility in life-and-death contests are really the reason he is able to escape Voldemort in their graveyard battle. If that seems far-fetched, it's important to note that Harry does well in the tournament only because of "charity" he receives (from those who want him dead—Moody/Crouch Jr. and Bagman), and only escapes Voldemort because of charity (from Voldemort's victims—those who are already dead). Although he's been tempted to take the low road of advantage in the tournament tasks rather than fighting the other champions, Harry refuses every time, and therefore he is equal to Voldemort's wiles because of his virtue.

THE REBIRTHING PARTY: LESSONS IN SPIRITUAL COMBAT

Goblet of Fire has its crucible scene in a graveyard where Voldemort is reborn in a mockery of everything sacred to Christians. A close look at what the Dark Lord calls his "Rebirthing Party" shows it to be a Black Mass.

A Black Mass is the demonic mockery of traditional Christian liturgy and sacramental worship. A Black Mass inverts everything that is sacred; death and darkness trump life and light. In the magic potion and ceremony that Voldemort orchestrates as black magician-priest, all the Christian sacraments are turned on their head, with demonic consequences:

- The Eucharist, or life-giving body and blood of God, are mocked in the potion's requirements of the blood of an enemy, flesh of the servant, and bone of the father (inverting blood of the Savior, flesh of the Master, and Spirit of the Father).
- The baptismal font and immersion in the name of Father, Son, and Holy Spirit are turned qualitatively inside out in the Voldemort baby's immersion in the cauldron with three magical, physical ingredients (and the "old man" rather than the "new man" or "babe in Christ" rising from the font).
- Confession, or the sacrament of reconciliation, occurs after (instead of before) this Black Mass and "old man" baptism—and the black arts priest neither forgives nor absolves the Death Eaters' sins and unworthiness but demands eye-for-an-eye service.

- Consecration of priests and disciples has its carnival mirror image in the blessing of Wormtail and the promised ordination and reward of Voldemort's true servants (and excommunication or murder of those who have broken faith with him).
- The Liturgy of the Word, or sermon, is mocked in Voldemort's edifying lesson and instruction to his disciples concerning his passion and resurrection.
- The mystery of Christian burial is turned on its head by the graveyard of a church becoming a birthplace of devils rather than a resting place for those hopeful of an authentic resurrection from the dead.

Harry not only witnesses the death of his friend and this series of demonic desecrations of holy things, he is part of it because his blood, made magically powerful by the sacrificial death and love of his mother, is necessary to the potion (another inversion of the Eucharist). And yet Harry decides to stand and fight as the image of his father. This steadfastness in faith, despite the darkness and perversion surrounding him, recalls his victory in the Chamber of Secrets and is the cause of Harry's consequent epiphany (realization of truth) and theophany (realization of God) in battle.[1]

This courage in making a choice, wrapped up with the love of the father, invites the golden light and inspiring phoenix song that envelope him when he locks wands with Voldemort. We find in *Fantastic Beasts* that phoenix song is "reputed to increase the courage of the pure in heart and to strike fear into the hearts of the impure."[2] We've already noted that in *Chamber of Secrets* this song is a symbol of the Holy Spirit, and the Trinity is again evident in the Light cage: The association with Dumbledore and the voice from the phoenix song suggest the words from the Father at Jesus' baptism (see Matthew

3:13-17), the phoenix feathers in the wand as a phoenix represent Christ, and the song with its effects points to the Holy Spirit.

Harry only experiences this symbolic epiphany of the Trinity because he is pure of heart. Again, in every task of the tournament, in every difficulty with close friends and media, he has stood courageously on the side of the truth rather than going for the easy win, quick fix, or safe path. As modern day Aesop's fables, the Harry Potter books seem to be telling us that it is not study, your special external preparations, or even your piety that save you in the end. Rather, it is your internal quality—the courage, love, and virtue within—that determines your receptivity to the graces that will save you in spiritual warfare.

If you think I overstate the case, please note that Harry's one-on-one combat with Voldemort in the graveyard (as in the earlier books) is a textbook illustration of how a Christian should face his or her three enemies: the world, the flesh, and the devil. Here's a closer look at the steps to face these enemies, with examples especially drawn from *Chamber of Secrets* and Harry's battle at the Rebirthing Party in *Goblet of Fire*:

- Recognize and name the enemy.
- Recognize your helplessness to combat this spiritual foe on your own.
- Confess your loyalty to the good.
- Look for the graces of the Trinity in the Holy Spirit.
- And finally, work these providential graces as best you can to overcome the enemy.

Throughout the Harry Potter series, combat and sports are used as metaphors for spiritual warfare. Through this, we learn the martial virtues of selfless sacrifice, bravery, and courageous combat—

the three virtues Voldemort tells Harry his parents displayed at their deaths.[3] I believe the author has chosen to connect sports to the spiritual because she is aware that sports and warfare have supplanted the Western church in the hearts and minds of many as places for masculine initiation and heroic virtue. Nonetheless, through these play and mortal battles, we can see the truths of the church and the greater battle against a foe who wants our spiritual death as much as our physical death.

In this, *Goblet of Fire* is no different from the other books of the series; where it differs is in the breadth of the effect that Harry's purity of heart has. We have seen in each book how our preparations and personal choices shape the outcome of our personal struggles with evil; in *Goblet of Fire*, we can see the larger consequences of this personal struggle for our friends and the world. Harry has not only survived, but his victory in escape has mobilized and inspired all the white hats to take on Voldemort. So, too, our pursuit of spiritual perfection, however private and personal, ennobles and enlightens the world.

THE GOBLET OF FIRE

Dumbledore took out his wand and tapped three times upon the top of the casket. The lid creaked slowly open. Dumbledore reached inside it and pulled out a large, roughly hewn wooden cup. It would have been entirely unremarkable had it not been full to the brim with dancing blue-white flames.[4]

Dumbledore tells us that "the champions will be chosen by an impartial selector: the Goblet of Fire" (chapter 16). Moody later describes it as "a very powerful magic object" (chapter 17). Is this a clever invention of Rowling's?

Well, yes and no. No, it has a referent in medieval legend, but yes,

Rowling has changed it a bit to suggest a specific meaning to that legendary piece. In Arthurian legend, the magical object that selected those champions worthy to behold it was the Holy Grail.

The Holy Grail, however, isn't a magical object like a Sneak-o-scope or Foe glass that detects defects in people. It has its power because it is the Communion cup of Christ's Last Supper; others say it caught the blood of Christ as he was crucified. Legend has it that it was brought by Joseph of Arimathea to England, at that time the most distant outpost of the Roman Empire. Readers of the Arthurian tales know that it could be found only by the most pure of heart (notably, Sirs Perceval and Galahad).

Rowling has made some interesting changes. The Grail of legend is silver, and it is sometimes represented more as a platter than what we would call a goblet. Her large, roughly hewn wooden cup is a Grail suggested by *Indiana Jones and the Last Crusade*. (Do you remember how Harrison Ford picks up a simple cup in a room full of ornate chalices, pointing to the link between the plain, earthenware cup and the Nazarene *carpenter*?)

But the more interesting changes are the casket and the flames. The flames might be a touch to satirize the Olympic torch, but the casket makes me think she is referring to what is inside a Communion cup: the body and blood of Christ. Traditional Christians say pre-Communion prayers that refer to their Savior's life-giving body and blood as fire:

> *If thou wishest, O man, to eat the Body of the Master, approach in fear, lest thou be scorched, for it is fire. (Didactic verses)*

> *Let the live coal of Thy Most Holy Body and Blood be for the sanctification and enlightenment and strengthening of my humble soul and body. (First Prayer of Saint John Chrysostomos)*

And rejoicing and trembling at once, I who am straw partake of fire; and strange wonder! I am ineffably bedewed, like the bush of old. (Prayer of Saint Symeon the New Theologian)

Behold I approach for Divine Communion. O Creator, let me not be burnt by communicating, for Thou art fire which burneth the unworthy; but purify me from every stain. (Saint Symeon Metaphrastes)

Thou hast ravished me with longing, O Christ, and with Thy divine love Thou hast changed me. But burn up with spiritual fire my sins and make me worthy to be filled with delight in Thee. (Communion Troparion)

The Goblet of Fire in the fourth book title is a fictional Holy Grail. However, Rowling's working title until shortly before the book went to press was *Harry Potter and the Doomspell Tournament.* I think the title was changed so the tournament would have a more Trinitarian feel (the Triwizard Tournament)—and so the title would point to the overarching meaning of the book.

The strangest characteristic of the fire in this Goblet is that it is a nonconsuming fire (the cup, remember, is made of wood, not clay). Applicants throw pieces of parchment into these flames, and the fire does not burn them. Though it may seem a stretch to modern Americans, most Christians can't help but note its parallels with the nonconsuming fire of the burning bush on Mount Sinai, the purifying flames of what Catholic believers call purgatory, and the glory or love of God, represented in the iconographic halo or nimbus in sacred art. All these are signatures or correspondences with God's Word, which became man as Christ.

Goblet of Fire is named for an object that appears in only one of its thirty-seven chapters and plays a small, mechanical part in the drama of the story, as compared to, say, the Triwizard Tournament or Voldemort's return. Its remarkable Christian meaning, however, makes it an apt title, and we will see its meaning and appropriateness echoed in the title of the fifth book in the series, *Harry Potter and the Order of the Phoenix.*

15

DARK NIGHT
OF THE SOUL

Christian keys to Harry Potter
and the Order of the Phoenix

I thought the release of *Goblet of Fire* had been a big deal. Compared to the release of *Harry Potter and the Order of the Phoenix, Goblet of Fire's* publication was a nonevent. Five million copies of *Order of the Phoenix* were sold in the first twenty-four hours of its availability. No one in the publishing industry expected this record to be broken— until the sixth book, *Half-Blood Prince,* was released, and incredibly, the record was shattered.

Order of the Phoenix, though, as popular as it is, disappointed millions of fans who wanted another *Chamber of Secrets* or *Goblet of Fire.* Sixty-five percent of fans who registered their opinion on a MuggleNet.com poll that first weekend said they did not like the book. I suspect the disappointed percentage was higher among younger fans and adult readers who were hoping for a light read at the beach.

They were disappointed because, frankly, *Order of the Phoenix* is a heavy read from beginning to end—what my Latin students called a "real downer." Harry is anything but lovable; he opens the book by bullying Dudley and screaming at Ron and Hermione. By book's end he has raised the stakes by tearing apart Dumbledore's office and shouting rude remarks at the headmaster. I was buried in electronic owls (e-mails) from fans and reporters within thirty-six hours of the book's release, asking me to explain what the "new Harry" was about.

What I told them was essentially this: The clue to understanding the "new Harry" in *Order of the Phoenix* is first to understand how *consistent* the fifth book is with the first four books, despite the seeming changes in tone and direction.

Note, for example, that this book keeps to the pattern of alternating extrovert books with introvert books. The themes of *Order of the Phoenix*, too, are the themes developed in the first four books. Pride and Prejudice—as embodied in the nightmarish High Inquisitor Dolores Umbridge—takes a front place in the book's meaning. Choice, change, and destiny continue on as themes as well. Harry learns at long last of his destiny as the prophesied vanquisher (or victim) of the Dark Lord, although he learns too late to avert an unnecessary tragedy. The theme of love over death, as detailed in chapters five and seven, also takes on new depth in *Order of the Phoenix*. Dumbledore tells Harry that his ability to vanquish the Dark Lord—the incarnation of the absence of life and love (and therefore, of death)—is in his tremendous capacity for love.

The structures of the first four books also return in *Order of the Phoenix*. All the elements we are accustomed to find in Harry's annual trip to Hogwarts continue according to formula despite the many changes at the school. And again we have an alchemical Great Work where the beginning reflects the end and the end is the inversion of the beginning.

But there is change beginning to end, too, and quite a remark-able change at that. On Privet Drive at the beginning of the book, Harry is hot and dry (or choleric, angry), as is the whole world he experiences, where there is a drought and heat wave. At book's end, however, after Harry's tantrum and his lesson about the prophecy, he is changed. Here Harry is described as cold and moist: "The sun had fallen before Harry realized that he was cold. He got up and returned to the castle, wiping his face on his sleeve as he went."[1]

His face is wet from tears, and we soon learn in his exchange with Luna that he is capable of more than anger and self-pitying grief. "An odd feeling rose in Harry—an emotion quite different from the anger and grief that filled him since Sirius's death. It was a few moments before he realized that he was feeling sorry for Luna."[2] The transformation of Harry in *Order of the Phoenix* from hot, dry, and angry to cold, wet, pitying, and even compassionate signals the most important change in him since his discovery that he was a wizard in *Sorcerer's Stone*.

I think it is the agony of this chrysalis that creates the most dis-comfort and disappointment for readers of *Order of the Phoenix*. As we touched on in chapter 4, *Order of the Phoenix* includes the three stages of the alchemical Great Work but focuses on the black stage, or nigredo, and as one might expect from these colorings, it is a dark business.

Lyndy Abraham's *Dictionary of Alchemical Imagery* describes the nigredo as:

The initial black stage of the opus alchymicum in which the body of the impure metal, the matter for the Stone, or the old outmoded state of being is killed, putrefied, and dissolved into the original substance of creation, the prima materia, in order that it may be renovated and reborn in a new form.[3]

Citing the alchemists' dependence on Christ's teaching—"Verily, verily, I say unto you, Except a corn of wheat fall into the ground and die, it abideth alone: but if it die, it bringeth forth much fruit" (John 12:24, KJV)—Abraham concludes:

> *The beginning of spiritual realization is always accompanied by some kind of sacrifice or death, a dying to the old state of things, in order to make way for the new insight and creation. Burckhardt observed that the turning away of the outer world to the inner to face the shadow of the psyche is frequently experienced as a nox profunda, before the dawning of the new light of illumination. The nigredo is a difficult phase, but only through experiencing it can the adept gain the wisdom and humility necessary for illumination.*[4]

Order of the Phoenix is Harry's dark night of the soul, or nigredo, in which everything in his world is either turned on its head or taken from him. What is left of Harry by book's end? He is not a Quidditch player, he is not enamored of Cho Chang, he is not distinct from Voldemort (the man he must kill or be killed by), he is no longer the son of a hero and of a "match made in heaven," he no longer overshadows Ron and Hermione in all things outside the classroom, he can no longer think of Privet Drive and his life at Hogwarts as separate realms without overlap or confusion (Hogwarts has been revealed as a paradise that can become a hell almost overnight), and he is no longer a hero in the public mind or able to play the hero in crisis without self-doubts. After Sirius's death—the climax of the nigredo being poetically expressed as the "death of Black" after a year in the House of Black—Harry is a shattered person. He knows the prophecy that set the events of his life in motion and that will shape his end, but the process of his breakdown in the grievous shadow (the meaning of *Dolores Umbridge*) of his fifth year leaves him unable to know who he is or what he wants.

Harry could not stand this, he could not stand being Harry anymore. . . .
He had never felt more trapped inside his own head and body, never wished
so intensely that he could be somebody—anybody—else. . . .

Whenever he was in company, he wanted to get away, and when he was
alone he wanted company. . . . Perhaps the reason he wanted to be alone
was because he had felt isolated from everybody since his talk with Dumble-
dore. An invisible barrier separated him from the rest of the world. He
was—he had always been—a marked man. It was just that he had never
really understood what that meant. . . . [5]

Harry has been broken down to a formless condition akin to the
prime matter of the alchemists in order to be able to understand
himself exclusively in the light of the prophecy. He struggles at
water's edge in the sunshine to come to grips with the fact that his
life must include, or end in, murder. Everything in his life will come
down to his ability to vanquish Voldemort—his "old man"—or his
failure to meet this destiny.

Why does this put readers off? Because in living through the
nigredo with Harry, as closely as we all identify with him, *we are
stripped down ourselves*. With Harry, we are reduced to our fundamental decision in life: Do I live a life of love for the "new man" and
for the Christ in me, or do I appease the "old man" and live with
death until my biological death seals my choice? This is a decision
few readers are delighted to be confronted with in any circum-
stance—and certainly not when reading a diversionary, supposedly
children's novel!

If the language of alchemy and Christianity makes your eyes go
glossy, look at it as a psychology course. We can understand the
"old man" as "dad," the way we use the phrase in common speech.
Order of the Phoenix is, in large part, about Harry's coming to terms

with his being the heir of his biological father, James. He is, it seems, living both *in* James's shadow and *as* James's shadow; note that at the beginning of the book Harry's behavior toward Dudley is not much different from James's bullying of Snape. Harry confronts this image of what he is becoming, rejects it, and then experiences the consequences of this rejection—the death of his father-shadow in the death of his godfather Sirius.

Neville in many ways is Harry's twin. Both were born at the same time, have similarly heroic parents, were effectively orphaned by Voldemort, and are linked in the prophecy. Neville goes through a similar break with his past when, in combat with the Death Eaters, he breaks his father's wand. Neville's grandmother has always told Neville he doesn't measure up to his father; by breaking his dad's wand, Neville is free to be his own man with his own wand.

Likewise, at the end of *Order of the Phoenix* Harry has been stripped of his ideas of himself and has further rid himself of his obligation to live as the image of his father. The only thing he is given to replace this no-longer-living psychological matrix is his revealed destiny as Voldemort's vanquisher or victim. Dumbledore explains that his identity as vanquisher lies in his capacity for love. Harry must decide between his old identity, the "old man" and image of James, or this "new man" of love, a power that is not his own and that he does not understand.

Order of the Phoenix ends with this question unresolved, although it seems unlikely that Harry will be able to deny his prophesied destiny now that it has been revealed to him. The book is a difficult experience for the reader because we identify with Harry as his old self-understanding is being stripped from him and as he is angry at the process (and at it taking so long!). The ending, in which he is shown his new identity (one he has already taken on at least in part as leader of Dumbledore's army), is stunning to us, even though we can see that the *nigredo* has prepared him for it.

Why are we stunned and uncomfortable with what Harry has experienced in *Order of the Phoenix?* I believe it's because we live in a culture without rites of transition from childhood to adulthood (unless taking the SAT or a driver's license test qualifies as a rite of passage). The United States is largely a commercial, desire-driven country in which children become independent children rather than autonomous adults. *Order of the Phoenix* is the story of a boy who is burnt to a crisp and then rises from the ashes as a new man, conscious of his prophesied destiny beyond his birthright to conquer death by love. Though all human beings are called to this destiny and to a decision to make this destiny the focus of our lives, few do so because of the demeaning distractions and diversions of our time.

This is suggested by the Disillusionment Charm used by Moody. By "disillusioning" the boy, the Auror makes Harry essentially invisible before their long flight to London from Privet Drive. The charm makes Harry a "human chameleon" indistinguishable from his surroundings. We would probably have called this an Illusionment Charm rather than a Disillusionment Charm, but the spell is well named. Being able to see through ourselves and see only those things external to us that shape us is disillusionment or enlightenment of a kind, because the forms we take on as our identity *are* delusion or illusion; we are, objectively speaking, really only transparencies of our environment, our heritage, and the accumulation of such influences over time. *Order of the Phoenix* is a book-length disillusionment for Harry to rid himself of his self-illusions and to prepare him for the revelation of who he *really* is at bottom: the destined vanquisher or victim of the Dark Lord, *as are we all.*[6]

Harry Potter and the Order of the Phoenix is a disturbing book for this and other reasons. The most important of these is the primary place love is given. This book nearly beats its readers over the head with love, and since few of us are as loving as we'd like to hope, it disturbs us.

Some notable "love moments" in *Order of the Phoenix* include:

- Dumbledore tells Harry that his grief is a reflection of his love.
- Dumbledore clarifies for Harry that the prophesied power of Voldemort's vanquisher—"the power the Dark Lord knows not"—is love.
- Harry learns that the sacrificial love of his mother lives on in the "bond of blood" he has with her via Aunt Petunia.
- Hagrid models sacrificial love in his care for Grawp, his half brother.
- Harry is victorious over Voldemort via his love for Sirius.
- Harry is unable to use an Unforgivable Curse effectively.

We learned in *Goblet of Fire* from Moody/Crouch Jr. that there are three Unforgivable Curses, the use of which means an automatic life sentence in Azkaban. These three curses call to mind the unforgivable sin of speaking against the Holy Spirit (Matthew 12:32; Mark 3:29; Luke 12:10). Let's look at how each of these curses is "speaking against the Holy Spirit":

Avadra Kedavra: The Killing Curse, a combination of the common-place "abracadabra" and "I have a cadaver," takes a life. The wizard who uses it supplants God as the giver and taker of life.
Crucio: The Cruciatus Curse tortures its object with excruciating pain until the curse is lifted. The curse itself means literally "I crucify (you)." This points to the fact that cruel treatment of

our fellow human beings translates to cruel treatment of God (Matthew 25:40).

Imperio: The Imperius Curse is Latin for "by command" or a variant of impero, which means "I give orders (to you)." This curse supplants the principal gift of God to man, his free will, by the will of the wizard performing the curse. Though not as damaging to the physical person as the other two curses, the Imperius Curse is the greater sin against the Holy Spirit.

The reason these curses are unforgivable is not so much in the nature of the curses themselves as it is in the *spiritual condition* the witch or wizard must be in to perform them correctly: one of willful separation from God and the good. The righteous can say the words, but the curses will lack the power they have when they are performed by the unrestrainedly wicked. Even in righteous anger, Harry, as a vehicle of love in the world, cannot sin against the Holy Spirit in this way. His connection with the good prohibits him from effectively using weapons of darkness to defeat Voldemort or his Death Eaters, as we see in the battles at the end of *Order of the Phoenix* and *Half-blood Prince.*[7]

All these instances of the power and qualities of love remind us that we as individuals are not as loving as we are commanded to be (John 15:12), but that we embrace advantage and death to greater or lesser degrees. Harry's struggle to embrace his prophesied destiny as the Dark Lord's vanquisher through love and light is the *human* struggle to do the same with the darkness in our fallen, hardened hearts.

Our discomfort with *Order of the Phoenix* might be summarized as our resistance to the demands of Christian life. As we watch Harry's childish ideas of himself dissolve in the *nigredo* during his fifth year at Hogwarts, we are confronted by our own need to renounce the world and its claims on us to follow Christ. In Harry's struggles with obedience in learning Occlumency, we experience our own resistance to watch over our heart, mind, and tongue, although we know it's necessary in order to keep them free of demonic temptation and sin. Reading about the Bond of Blood that protects Harry, we must examine our own understanding of the bond of blood we have in Christ by his sacrifice and the Eucharist he left for us to preserve us in that bond. And in the death of Sirius Black and Harry's agony over his part in it, we are reminded of our accountability for the fallen nature of the world and of our failure to pursue our destiny in Christ by difficult, righteous choices.

Order of the Phoenix contains the most explicitly Christian references of the series so far. Harry gets a glimpse beyond the veil—a reference both to the veil of the temple and the Shack in Lewis's *Last Battle*—to an afterlife where the righteous will meet again. We also see the mysterious power behind the door, which is both "more wonderful and more terrible than death, than Human intelligence, than forces of nature."[8] This power burns the unworthy and protects the beloved (see the end of *Sorcerer's Stone*): a reflection of God's love, also known as his judgment, mercy, and glory. And we find the answer to the riddle of death and our fallen nature in Love himself, he who is of two natures but one in essence with the Father.

Even the title of the book, *Harry Potter and the Order of the Phoenix*, resonates with our Christian faith. The Order of the Phoenix is the band of magical folk allied to combat Voldemort's Death Eaters. As we've already seen, the term *Death Eaters* points to antagonism toward Christians, who are commanded by God, who is Life, to be "Life Eaters" in remembrance of him. But the Order of the Phoenix points to the Christian life in more ways than just its opposition to Voldemort's Death Eaters.

The word *order* is a religious term, referring to a group with a specific vocation (until modern times almost always primarily con-templative) within the church. That this order is "of the Phoenix," a traditional symbol both of the end of alchemy and of Christ him-self, highlights this otherworldly meaning.

And what does the phoenix do? As we see Fawkes do in spectac-ular fashion at the end of *Order of the Phoenix,* the living symbol of Christ swallows the Death Curse of the enemy, dies in flames (the *nigredo*), renouncing the world and life itself in sacrificial love for its brother—and in the hope of being born again in Christ's image, rising from the dead. We are called to this end through Scripture, through the example of the saints in Christian tradition, and through the remarkable example of Harry Potter in this imaginative literature. With the rest of the reading world, I applauded the author of this edifying book and rushed to read her next-to-last installment in the saga.

16

BAPTISM INTO A
SACRICIFIAL DEATH

Christian Keys to Harry Potter
and the Half-Blood Prince

Potter-mania was by no means exhausted after the release of the
fifth book and third movie of this popular series; if anything, the
book and movie only created a greater interest in the young wizard
from the UK. The sixth book, *Harry Potter and the Half-Blood Prince,*
when released in July 2005, had a first-run printing of more than
10 million hardcover copies in the United States alone—7 million
copies more than any book that was not by Joanne Rowling.

Fortunately, *Half-Blood Prince* disappointed very few fans and
only confirmed Rowling's place in the hearts of children and adult
readers. Unlike *Order of the Phoenix*, which was received as "mixed"
to "poor" at first but was eventually embraced by fandom as perhaps the best of the series, *Half-Blood Prince* has been a fan favorite
since it came out of the gates. Why? Well, for starters, it is a lot
less painful to read!

BLACK TO WHITE—PHEW!

As we have already seen, *Phoenix* is the alchemical reduction by fire of Harry from all his ego concerns. The alchemical *nigredo*, or "black work," however, ended with the death of Sirius Black and the closing of *Phoenix*. The opening of *Prince* had to be in a cold rain as the books entered the *albedo*, or alchemical "white work." *Half-Blood Prince* is the Potter novel in which Harry is purified for the final work of spiritual transformation by the immersion in cleansing waters and the dissolution of contraries in the story. This part of Harry's journey, comparatively speaking at least, is a lot of fun!

Snow, Booze, and Tears in the White Work

If you have a *Dictionary of Literary Alchemy* on hand, look up *white*, *ablution*, or *albedo*. What you'll find is a host of specific things to look for, including *luna*, the nighttime stars, the white lily, a swan, water, cold, and whiteness—anything pale, silvery, or white.

We learn in the opening pages of *Prince* that an unseasonable "chilly mist" pervades Britain this July, and cold, wet weather is the backdrop of the entire story. Rain, sleet, snow, and banks of mist are the rule for *Prince*. When Ron waves his wand "vaguely in the direction of the ceiling" near the book's end, it begins to snow.[1] This Harry Potter adventure, for the most part, takes place in the fog, near a body of water, or stepping in from wet weather.

The fluid in every scene isn't restricted to what's in the atmosphere. It's a rare chapter in *Half-Blood Prince* that doesn't include a drinking scene. From the two large glasses of whiskey that Cornelius Fudge conjures "out of thin air" for the Muggle Prime Minister in the opening chapter, the "bloodred wine" Snape pours for his guests in Spinner's End, and the glasses of "Madam

Rosmerta's finest oak-matured mead" Dumbledore serves the Dursleys on his visit to Privet Drive, to the poisoned mead that almost kills Ron on his birthday, the cooking sherry that Professor Trelawney drowns her professional sorrows in, and the bottles of elf-made wine that Professor Slughorn drinks with Hagrid after Aragog's funeral, it's a rare chapter in which Muggles and wizards aren't drinking strong spirits.

All this imbibing stops, however, with the twelve crystal goblets of emerald phosphorescent potion that Dumbledore drinks on the island in the cavern lake, which begins the climax of the alchemical drama.

In a book about purification and fluid, of course, everyone cries real tears (or at least has moistened eyes) somewhere in this drama. Some characters are crying because their love is unrequited, others weep because of fear or joy, and Dumbledore himself gets teary because he is touched by Harry's loyalty.[2] Even the hard-hearted characters cry openly at Dumbledore's death and funeral.

A Teen Romance with Spiritual Meaning?
Rowling's books are all detective fiction: largely about solving a mystery. This year's mystery is Draco's secret suicide mission from Lord Voldemort. In between this action, however, we are buried in teenage romance.

This is not any less appropriate to the subtext of the alchemical white stage than rain, booze, and tears. Ron and Hermione, alchemical sulphur and quicksilver, respectively, have in previous books been the "quarreling couple" of alchemy, whose differences and agreements have been the refining work of Harry's purification in drama. In *Prince*, after a comedy of misunderstandings and attempts to show up the other, these two at last recognize their destiny together.

In fact, the book ends very much like a Shakespeare comedy or Austen novel, with every couple coming together at long last for a happy ending of sorts. Bill and Fleur's union is finally blessed by Mrs. Weasley's tears, Tonks and Lupin hold hands at the funeral, Harry and Ginny become the long foreshadowed Arthur and Guinevere, and Ron and Hermione are the crowned red king and white queen of Harry's alchemical dreams.

The action of the book, then, is ablution, and the scrubbing is the attraction and repulsion of contraries that are finally resolved. This is not a painless process, as those who have been scrubbed clean by their mother remember. But it sure beats being reduced to a cinder from merciless heat, as we as readers were in the fifth Harry Potter book.

Washing Is about Purification

When you bleach, wash, and scrub your favorite white dress shirt, it comes out brilliantly white, doesn't it? And we have white images galore in this white stage book: Slughorn's magnificent mustache; the snow that falls indoors and out for months at a time; the beautiful, blonde Luna in "spangled silver robes" at the Christmas party; the dreadful Inferi living in the cavern lake; the white flame, white smoke, silver Phoenix Patronus, and white tomb at Dumbledore's funeral. This book needed a white cover.

And few people blush in this book. Everyone turns white, pale, or gray at one point or another. Tonks goes colorless; Draco is white or gray; everyone who is startled, angry, tired, or otherwise emotionally elevated is "white."

But the whitest part of the book is the reappearance of Albus Dumbledore, whose first name in Latin means "white" or "resplendent." Largely absent in *Phoenix*, the headmaster is never very far from Harry's mind in this book. In *Prince*, Dumbledore gives five tutorials, all of which are instructions in the life and ways of Lord Voldemort. After he reveals the ways of the evil one and what must be done to defeat him, Dumbledore the alchemist marvels at the love within Harry and at his purity:

> *"You are protected, in short, by your ability to love!" said Dumbledore loudly. "The only protection that can possibly work against the lure of power like Voldemort's! In spite of all the temptation you have endured, all the suffering, you remain pure of heart, just as pure as you were at the age of eleven, when you stared into a mirror that reflected your heart's desire, and it showed you only the way to thwart Lord Voldemort, and not immortality or riches. Harry, have you any idea how few wizards could have seen what you saw in that mirror? Voldemort should have known then what he was dealing with, but he did not!*
>
> *"But he knows it now. You have flitted into Lord Voldemort's mind without damage to yourself, but he cannot possess you without enduring mortal agony, as he discovered in the Ministry. I do not think he understands why, Harry, but then, he was in such a hurry to mutilate his own soul, he never paused to understand the incomparable power of a soul that is untarnished and whole."*[3]

Proclaiming Harry's purity and love as his best weapons against the Dark Lord, the White Wizard then takes Harry on a trip to destroy a Horcrux of Lord Voldemort—Harry's baptism by water and fire.

A STORY LIKE ALL OTHER STORIES

But I'm well ahead of myself. *Half-Blood Prince* is very different from the previous books in this series because of the alchemical step it represents in Harry's "Everyman" journey to spiritual perfection. These differences, though, should not obscure the fact that this is, indeed, a Harry Potter book, in every way like the other Potter books.

By this I don't just mean we have the same characters at the same school with the same likes and dislikes, however true this is. *Prince* also has all the themes, formula structures, and traditional Christian symbolism that mark Harry Potter as surely as his lightning bolt–shaped scar.

The Harry Potter Formula Checklist

Let's run through our Harry Potter checklist. Mystery? As we've already seen, our mystery is in trying to figure out what terrible secret mission Draco has been assigned by the angry Lord Voldemort. Check this off the list.

Narrative traction? Quarreling Ron and Hermione, Lord Voldemort's story in tutorial flashbacks with Dumbledore. Two checks.

Hero's journey from Privet Drive to King's Cross? With the exception of the ending that seems to have multiple symbols of Christ, saving Harry from death again and again but without a trip to King's Cross, everything is in place here, too.

Is the magical world still divided neatly along the Gryffindor/Slytherin axis? This remains the conflict at the heart of the books—it's still either Voldemort's way or the selfless way of moral courage, but the world isn't neatly divided (outside of Hogwarts, anyway) between white hats and Death Eaters. We meet even more politicos and worldly types among the witches and wizards who are nominally opposed to Voldemort but resist him with the methods of a Death Eater.

And the four themes that define this seven-book series—change, choice, prejudice, and love's victory over death—are all here too, as we have reviewed in previous chapters on these themes. Love and death merit an extra word.

Death: Horror of Horcrux

The question that haunts Harry Potter readers is, What is the link between Harry and Lord Voldemort? The mystery of both Harry's survival of the dreaded *Avadra Kedavra* curse as an infant and Voldemort's survival of the rebounded curse is the key. We take a big step forward in understanding this mystery in *Half-Blood Prince*, in which we learn of the existence of Voldemort's Horcruxes. These Horcruxes also play a key role in developing the theme of death, as well as love's victory over death—a large part of the book's meaning.

The Horcrux is "the word used for an object in which a person has concealed part of their soul. . . . You split your soul, you see," says Slughorn, "and hide part of it in an object outside the body. Then, even if one's body is attacked or destroyed, one cannot die, for part of the soul remains earthbound and undamaged."[4] The "horror" in Horcrux is that splitting the soul is only possible "by an act of evil—the supreme act of evil. By committing murder. Killing rips the soul apart. The wizard intent upon creating a Horcrux would use the damage to his advantage: He would encase the torn portion" by a spell into an object.[5]

The nightmare of Voldemort's immortality experiments is that he has six Horcruxes outside of his body for a total of seven soul fragments that must be destroyed.

The word *Horcrux* is an interesting combination of Latin and French derivations. *Hor-crux* from the Latin would be "frightening or horrible" (*horreo*) and "cross" (*crux*); rather than finding the way to immortality in the lifesaving sacrifice of Christ, the Horcrux accomplishes the task through murder.

Although the word *Horcrux* is probably a Rowling invention, the idea of encasing part of the soul into a physical object apart from the body is not an innovation in literature, folk tales, or myths. It reflects obliquely the Christian teaching on the nature of a saint's incorruptible body at death (i.e., the grace-filled power of relics).

Rowling's brilliant spin on this literary cliché, however, is to say the soul is "rent" by sin and "split" by the greatest of sins against love for others (their murder, physically or spiritually). Lord Voldemort, the arch villain, pursues immortality apart from God and the Cross by pouring his soul into physical objects apart from his body. In this, Voldemort is simultaneously a materialist and a dualist—and no longer human, as Dumbledore says, because he fails to understand the power of a human being who is whole, an integer of body and soul, and pure, which is to say "not rent or split."[6]

To destroy Voldemort, then, Harry must find and destroy the four remaining Horcruxes and Lord Voldemort *while at the same time* remaining "pure of heart." Dumbledore warns Harry that, even after the Horcruxes are destroyed, "while his soul may be damaged beyond repair, his brain and his magical powers remain intact. It will take uncommon skill and power to kill a wizard like Voldemort even without his Horcruxes."[7] This power, Dumbledore tells Harry, is Harry's love.

Two things are especially worthy of note here. First, Voldemort's path to escape death (his name meaning, literally, "flight from death") is clearly the wrong one—a path that the reader is taught to see as an atrocity. This way to immortality is the way of ego preservation, identification with material things, disregard for the body as an integral aspect of the human person, and quite literally the rendering of the soul for power and personal advantage. Looking at the monster that the soul-twisted and torn Voldemort has become, we see in story form the answer to Christ's question: "What shall it profit a man, if he shall gain the whole world, and lose his own soul?" (Mark 8:36, KJV).

In contrast, Harry the hero does not fear physical death. If anything, he seems more than a bit reckless with his life when he gets caught up in what Hermione calls his "saving-people-thing."[8] His close attachment to his ego concerns was largely broken in his fifth year at Hogwarts, when almost every activity he loved and the ideas he identified with were taken from him or spoiled. He is a young man who loves his friends, loves the good, and loves romantically as well. More than anything else, he is determined to do the right thing, whatever it costs him personally.

This contrast brings me to my second point about the Horcrux. What does the reader of this Harry Potter novel come away with as the meaning of death in these books? A Catholic friend in Canada and a young sophist in a Louisiana seminary both wrote me to say that Dumbledore's death "sends a disturbing, confusing moral message" to children about euthanasia (they believe Dumbledore planned his own death). My earnest friends have missed entirely Rowling's point: You have a soul. The purity of your soul and its capacity for love are your greatest strengths. Sin and evil rend your soul and diminish you toes to nose. Invest your soul in the good and in those you love, not material objects. Love and an "untarnished and whole" soul will defeat death and his minions.

Rowling does not argue for the soul's existence, and she does not didactically offer Harry's way as superior to Lord Voldemort's twisted path. Her story, however, makes care for the soul and love of the good, true, and beautiful all things we want for ourselves. She is stealing golden wheelbarrows here—and wheeling loads of edifying truths into our heart.

What we have learned about death in *Half-Blood Prince* is that the death we must fear is a spiritual one. If we care for our souls and work to be as loving as we can, we may cheat death and those who fear and serve the Dark Lord.

FORMULA ENDING: WHO OR WHAT IS THE CHRIST SYMBOL IN *HALF-BLOOD PRINCE?*

The four principal themes—change, choice, prejudice, and death—then, can all be checked off our Rowling formula master list. We know too that she is still using the alchemical formula in making *Half-Blood Prince* the "white stage" novel. What remains? Her hero journey formula ends every year with Harry's resurrection from the dead in the presence of a traditional symbol of Christ and with the revelation of a bad guy who seemed good (or vice versa).

This year we have both, in spades. In fact, Harry seems to be saved from death by *three* different Christ figures, and we seem to have learned at last the real master and consequent allegiance of Severus Snape. Let's look first at the end of Harry's journey, his near death, and his being saved again.

Every year after the mystery has come to a crisis, Harry and his friends confront the bad guys underground, he dies a figurative death, and he survives because of love in the presence of a symbol of Christ. He comes to terms with the battle's meaning, a good guy is revealed as a bad guy (or vice versa), and everyone travels home on the Hogwarts Express to King's Cross Station. In *Half-Blood Prince*, we have all these elements except the train ride home (canceled because of the funeral), and several lifesaving events and symbols of Christ.

The symbol most like previous symbols is Buckbeak the hippogriff, who saves Harry from a seemingly murderous and unhinged Severus Snape. After a long chase from the top of the Astronomy Tower to the Hogwarts grounds (this year's descent underground), Harry lies helpless before Snape's wrath when the hippogriff swoops in with his razor-like claws to drive the former Potions Master out the gate.

Snape, too, hard as it may be for some to believe, must also be considered one of Harry's saviors in *Half-Blood Prince*. He saves Harry from the other Death Eaters, right after Harry makes his formulaic speech about death: *This must be it, the pain is too great, I must be dying.*

Snape, an unlikely Christ symbol, I'll admit, qualifies as such because of this rescue, because he is in fact the Half-Blood Prince—a pointer to the "Double Natured King," certainly—and because of his being the "great physician" in this year's adventure. He not only "stoppers Dumbledore's death" by sealing the arm wound Dumbledore received when destroying the ring Horcrux, but he also saves Draco Malfoy's life (and Harry from a trip to Azkaban) by sewing up the *Sectumsempra* Curse slash by singing the healing charm (shades of Aslan).

As interesting as Buckbeak and Snape are, however, I doubt they are really the saviors of this year's adventure. Albus Dumbledore rescues Harry in the cave, and his actions there and on the Astronomy Tower mark him as a powerful image of the Man-God beyond any concern about literary formula requirements and checklists.

Dumbledore at Half-Blood Prince's Stygian Lake

At the crisis of this year's mystery, Harry learns simultaneously that Draco Malfoy has succeeded in whatever project he has been working on all year in the Room of Requirement, that Dumbledore is ready to leave Hogwarts on a Horcrux search-and-destroy mission, and that it was Severus Snape who overheard the prophecy years before and told Voldemort about it. Pulled in three different directions by these revelations, Harry is of two minds as he leaves the castle with Dumbledore, which he does only after sending his friends on a mission to prevent Snape and Malfoy from carrying out an attack on Hogwarts in their absence.

Harry and the headmaster apparate from Hogsmeade to a cave. Once inside the cave, and after Dumbledore performs a necessary "crude" blood sacrifice, they gain entrance to a much larger cave that holds a vast lake of glass-smooth black water. They travel by magic boat to an island at the center of this Stygian lake, in which lives an army of magically animated corpses called *Inferi*.

At the center of this small island is a stone basin filled with a phosphorescent emerald-colored fluid that proves impenetrable to magic. Dumbledore is confident that the Horcrux they are seeking is at the bottom of this basin and decides he must drink the fluid to reveal the Horcrux. After extracting Harry's promise to force him to drink it all, he chokes down twelve chalices of the green fluid, screaming for mercy and death, and then collapses with a death rattle. Harry revives him and is unable to give him the water he requests until he dips the chalice into the lake, which brings the Inferi to the island to protect the Horcrux.

Harry, after some struggle with these living dead, resigns himself to death in the lake they are carrying him into. But Dumbledore rises from the ground and his seeming death and drives the Inferi away with a ring of fire. He grabs the locket in the basin, and they escape the island and the cavern lake, and apparate back to Hogsmeade. The headmaster, near collapse, is more than half carried by Harry from the cave but reassures Harry by telling him that he is not worried: "I am with you."

Let's review what happens in the cave.

- Dumbledore offers his blood sacrificially at the cave entrance.
- He drinks twelve cups of a green fluid and suffers horribly.
- He rises from death to turn back with warmth and light the Inferi who have captured Harry.
- He reassures Harry by expressing confidence in him with the magisterial, "I am with you."

Dumbledore himself calls the blood sacrifice "crude"—an obvious cue that this is Dumbledore's walk to Calvary. His drinking the twelve cups on the island, the center of darkness and death, represents his taking upon himself the totality (twelve being the number of a complete cycle) of sins and evil in the world. (Green, with few exceptions, in these stories is the color of Slytherin and the Dark Lord.) He suffers horribly and dies in his voluntary acceptance of the bitter cup (compare to Matthew 26:39). The headmaster rises from the dead and harrows the denizens of hell with light to save his disciple (compare to John 1:4 and Matthew 17:2). He reverses and echoes his early pronouncement of Harry being safe because "you are with me" with his "I am with you" (compare to Matthew 28:20 and John 17:21).

But though near death, Dumbledore flies from Hogsmeade on a rescue mission to Hogwarts, which he and Harry see upon their return is under the Dark Mark, the sign of death. On his arrival at the Astronomy Tower, which has been foretold will be his doom, he is disarmed and attacked by a student who has betrayed him to his enemies. He is merciful to the student, who mistakenly believes that he has the greatest wizard who ever lived at bay because he is wandless, and Dumbledore offers him forgiveness, sanctuary, and the freedom to choose to turn from evil and death of his own volition, uncoerced. Dumbledore is surrounded by tormentors before the boy can accept his love, and then Dumbledore is seemingly murdered by a friend and blasted from the Tower.

This morality play is not given with scriptural references within the story. I have to think, nonetheless, that few Christians struggle to see the parallels with Christ's loving, sacrificial death for us.

- Dumbledore comes to Hogwarts to die and to save its occupants from the rule of death that hovers over the castle.

- He is tormented by those he could destroy even without a wand or escape by Transfiguration, even though he is weakened from his suffering in the cave (Plato's allegory of the world).
- He is merciful, loving, and respectful of man's free will to accept or deny this mercy and love.
- He is betrayed by a disciple and murdered by those he has come to save.
- His death is, on the surface, ignominious, brutal, and senseless.

At Dumbledore's funeral, too, Rowling repeats the theme of Harry's safety being linked to Dumbledore's presence. Harry explains that Dumbledore may be dead but he is not gone, and that Harry's loyalties remain with the headmaster. But as we have seen, Harry may be Dumbledore's man by public confession, but he is not yet a Dumbledore man through and through, because of his prejudices and anger. In the last year of his Hogwarts adventures, I think we have to expect him to struggle from just being Dumbledore's image to being his likeness. This will be possible if he imitates Dumbledore in his choices.

Dumbledore has revealed to Harry that freedom exists primarily in our free will efforts to realize our destiny. Dumbledore's choices in his death are Christlike, and if Harry is to defeat Lord Voldemort with love, he will have to follow in his headmaster's footsteps.

Harry has been ascending the ladder of love that Plato described in *The Symposium*. The four Greek words for love are *storge* (affection), *philia* (friendship), *eros* (sexual or romantic love) and *agape* (selfless love). Harry has managed to climb from the family love he never knew at the Dursleys (but found at Hogwarts) to a romantic love with Ginny at the end of *Half-Blood Prince.* What is left for him to master is the selfless or sacrificial love that his mother showed in her choices while battling Voldemort and that Dumbledore showed in the cave and on the Tower.

CONCLUSION: MEANING OF *HALF-BLOOD PRINCE*

Every Harry Potter novel to date has been an allusion to Christ, and *Half-Blood Prince* is no exception. You do not need to be a theologian or even a Sunday-only Christian to make the leap from "Half-Blood Prince" to the "Double Natured King."

Half-Blood Prince, as the "white work" in the alchemical drama, is largely the story of Harry's immersion in water, purification of heart, and ultimately baptism into the sacrificial suffering and death of Albus Dumbledore—Rowling's symbol of the God-Man. Harry has, if you will, "put on Christ" (see Romans 6:3-12 and Galatians 3:27) but is not yet the "through and through" man of faith that he thinks he is. As he gathers and destroys the remaining Horcruxes in his seventh year, we will see if he has realized and taken to heart the power of love that can defeat death.

As these six books have revealed, in large part, faith in story form, and if my suspicions are correct, as the sacrificial love ending of the series will, I still marvel at the great gift these novels are to the world. Readers around the world are fully engaged and being shaped by images of love and sacrifice resonant of Christ and by a plotline based on the virtues of courage, loyalty, and purity.

I do not know how the story will end, but if every trip is more about the journey than the destination, I could not be more grateful for my time (and my children's time) with Harry and friends, wherever we wind up. Harry's remarkable popularity in my home and his unrivaled success in homes around the world speaks to the human heart, however many dragons may guard it, still having a God-shaped hole we long to fill.

Harry Potter is not the plug for this hole. In the best tradition of English culture and letters, however, reading Harry's adventures points us to and prepares us for the journey to the cure for our heart disease in the "real world." We can ask for no greater gift from our reading than the imaginative baptism we enjoy in *Half-Blood Prince*. The spiritually lame may not walk after finishing the Harry Potter novels, but every reader is engaged and edified by his adventures.[16]

17
THE POWER OF CHRISTIAN ARTISTRY

Keys to the future and legacy
of the Harry Potter series

In *Looking for God in Harry Potter*, I've tried to uncover the larger meaning of this popular book series and to help you determine if it is an edifying message for Christians.

After examining the structures, themes, predominant symbolism, and individual books, I've come to believe that the books are about love and death. Rowling's understanding and exposition of these large-as-life questions about the meaning of life are both consistent with Christian answers to these questions and written in implicitly Christian language. The Harry Potter books answer, in story form, the questions we have about what it means to be fully human.

In this last chapter, I'd like to make some predictions of what I think must happen in the last book of the series. I also hope to review the reasons we as Christians have to celebrate their great success. But first we need to hurdle the criticisms.

LOVING TO HATE HARRY

I need to speak to the critics first in this conclusion because many find it difficult to take the Harry Potter books seriously. Because they are supposedly children's books and because so many critics have said they are not quality reading material, it is easy to dismiss them. Harold Bloom of Yale has said they are "just slop." William Safire of the *New York Times* wrote that they are "unworthy of adult attention." A. S. Byatt tells us, "Ms. Rowling's magic world has no place for the numinous. It is written for people whose imaginative lives are confined to TV cartoons, and the exaggerated (more exciting, not threatening) mirror-worlds of soaps, reality TV and celebrity gossip."[1] Even writers and professors who claim to like the books often do not encourage readers to enjoy them except as cultural artifacts.

It is true that Rowling is not a Dickens or a Tolstoy or even an A. S. Byatt in her lyrical use of the language. Perhaps Stephen King is right that she is too dependent on adverbs to convey mood and tone; certainly she of all authors could be accused of suffering from "successful author syndrome," in which no editor dares to trim the prose, if only because the world has never known such a successful author. *Order of the Phoenix* may have shown signs of this (though, with this author, I wouldn't know where to begin cutting), but *Half-Blood Prince* was the tightest narrative trip since *Chamber of Secrets*.

Having said that, I rush to point out that her writing strengths and accomplishments in the series have been so neglected as to amount to something like willful blindness. As we've already noted, Harry Potter is growing in three dimensions year by year. He is growing physically, of course, but he is also growing in awareness as well as in spiritual capacity and depth. Rowling has reflected this growth remarkably in her exposition of the themes and in the perspective from which the stories are told.

Suman Gupta, in his otherwise unexceptional *Re-Reading Harry Potter*, makes this point well in his chapter "Repetition and Progression." He explains that the books (in the words of Alison Williams) "achieve a rare balance of repeating themes and increasing complexity. [Gupta] notes how the initial themes are introduced, then elaborated, developed and deepened at each repetition."[2] Rowling is masterfully repeating these themes, bringing more to light and from a greater depth at each repetition in each successive year.[3]

This is not the happy accident of formulaic writing. Note the perspective from which the stories are told. With only one or perhaps two exceptions, every chapter is told from what literature professors call third person limited omniscient view. Translated into English, that means we learn the story as if there is an elf with a Minicam on Harry's shoulder who is also able to see what is going on inside Harry's head. The story is not told by Harry (first person view) or from the view of the all-seeing narrator (third person omniscient view) but from Harry's limited perspective and his limited ability to comprehend what is going on around him.

We experience the stories, consequently, from Harry's changing ability to see and understand what is happening through his eyes. This view is usually growing but oftentimes blurred by emotion. The books are getting longer and more detailed because Harry is able to experience more as his comprehension expands. These changes are due to the remarkable requirements Rowling has placed on herself in writing a coming-of-age story from this particular perspective. We experience the themes in each book not only in light of the particular plot, but also in Harry's growing perspective and capacity—morally, intellectually, and spiritually.

Occam's razor is relevant here: "Explanations of unknown phe-

nomenon should be sought first among known quantities." I take
that to mean that when you cannot explain something unprecedented, look to the obvious answer first before stretching out for
the wild reason. Potter-mania is such an unprecedented phenomenon, many don't know how to take it. Some critics attempt to
explain it by saying that the Harry Potter books are so popular
because the books are so bad and people are so stupid.

I am not one to underestimate the dumbing-down influence of
television and popular culture in America. I do think, though,
that the more obvious and more charitable answer to the Potter-
mania question is that these books are so much better than other
books.

This is true not only in their accomplished narrative misdirection and tight plotting, but also in their meaning and Christian
themes. To grasp this requires an understanding of the fundamen-
tals of market economics and of why people read stories in the
first place.

The marketplace first. If a product sells phenomenally well, we
assume it meets a need or satisfies a previously unrecognized desire.
A car that gets one hundred miles to the gallon and costs less than
ten thousand dollars will sell well because it meets the need for
transportation that is not expensive to purchase or to run. Pretty
simple, really—success in the marketplace depends largely on meeting the needs of consumers.

What are the needs of fiction readers, young and old? The simple answer is, of course, entertainment. We read for diversion, distraction, or just for pleasure. This answer, though, raises another
question. Why does immersion in a story give us pleasure? It has
to do with human design, believe it or not.

Huston Smith, famous authority on the world's religions, tells
this story in *Why Religion Matters:*

At the Press Conference that the university mounted on [Saul Bellow's] arrival, one of the reporters asked him, "Mr. Bellow, you are a writer and we are writers. What's the difference between us?" Bellow answered, "As journalists, you are concerned with news of the day. As a novelist, I am concerned with news of eternity."[4]

People who read novels are looking for this eternal news. They look for it because, even in a profane and materialist culture—with, as one symbolist put it, "a low ceiling and a deep basement"—the human heart longs for some experience of the sacred. We find this experience of the sacred, according to Mircea Eliade, in our entertainments and especially in the books we read:

Nonreligious man in the pure state is a comparatively rare phenomenon, even in the most desacralized of modern societies. The majority of the "irreligious" still behave religiously even though they are not aware of the fact. We refer not only to modern man's many "superstitions" and "tabus," all of them magico-religious in structure. But the modern man who feels and claims that he is nonreligious still retains a large stock of camouflaged myths and degenerated rituals. . . .

A whole volume could be written on the myths of modern man, on the mythologies camouflaged in the plays that he enjoys, in the books that he reads. The cinema, that "dream factory," takes over and employs countless motifs—the fight between hero and monster, initiatory combats and ordeals, paradigmatic figures and images. . . . Even reading includes a mythological function, not only because it replaces the recitation of myths in archaic societies and the oral literature that still lives in the rural communities of Europe, but particularly because, through reading, the modern man succeeds in obtaining an "escape from time" comparable to the "emergence from time" effected by myths. Whether modern man "kills" time with a detective story

or enters such a foreign temporal universe as is represented by any novel,
reading projects him out of his personal duration and incorporates him into
other rhythms, makes him live in another "history."[5]

The great writers of fiction understand and embrace the fact
that their novels act as detailed little worlds that serve a *mythological*
function in a profane culture. In our culture—a culture in which
religious worship has been cast as "the opiate of the ignorant"—
fiction, sport, and popular entertainment touch us where we live,
feeding our innate hunger for some experience of a greater existence than our flat, mundane concerns.

This being the case, there must be something about the
Potter books that raises them above the great mass of books
being sold today, because they are obviously satisfying this need
more than their competitors. I believe this "something" is that
part of them connects with our desire for Christian content and
meaning.

It's been said that "all souls are Christian souls." Obviously, this
does not mean that everyone is a professing Christian; instead, it
points to the doctrine that says all men are made by God's creative
word and designed to receive that same word—because there is a
correspondence (amounting to identity) between human intellect
or logic and the Logos of God that created man and the world. It
is implicit in human design that we long for Christ and the experience of the Great Story.

Even in our post-Christian culture, consequently, it is possible
to see two truths in the great success of the Potter stories:

- The great mass of people, despite materialist immunizations
  and naturalist booster shots, still long for explicitly Christian
  spiritual experiences.

- The prevalent culture is so profane and bereft of what is good, true, and beautiful that our desire for these things is overwhelming when we are presented with what we crave.

Hence, Potter-mania. There are three reasons, then, why these books are so popular:

- They teach us traditional doctrines we long to hear.
- They give us some vicarious, imaginative experience of the truth of these doctrines.
- They deliver it all inside a wonderfully engaging, entertaining story.

Perhaps it seems like a stretch to say Harry Potter has taken the world by storm because the world wants desperately to experience Christian truths. I really believe that's the reason, however. We are designed for a relationship with our Creator. The language of this relationship that speaks most directly to the human heart is the imagery and symbols of the Christian church. And since our fallen humanity and culture restrict our ability to seek this relationship directly, we seek to satisfy our spiritual needs in our entertainments. Those entertainments that artfully retell the Christian story with the Christian answers to life's big questions are often the most popular because they meet the needs of the modern reader most effectively.

It is no accident, consequently, that the fiction of J. R. R. Tolkien, C. S. Lewis, and J. K. Rowling are the best sellers of our time. The books of these writers have more in common than just their popularity with readers of all ages and nationalities. These books all essentially disguise or hide theology within their stories.

Lewis explained why he did this in an essay called "Sometimes Fairy Stories May Say Best What's to Be Said." His concern with sharing his faith in story form was that readers, especially young readers, don't like preachy stories or transparent allegories. The secret to reaching the hearts of readers longing for Christian experience of some kind is to recast the story in fantasy. He wrote:

> But supposing that by casting all these things into an imaginary world, stripping them of their stained glass and Sunday school associations, one could make them for the first time appear in their real potency? Could one not thus steal past those watchful dragons? I thought I could.[6]

Many Potter fans believe that Rowling is well aware of these "watchful dragons" in our heart ever on the lookout for churchy messages (one assumes in order to chase them away with flaming dragon breath!). They point to the Hogwarts School motto, *"draco dormiens numquam titillandus,"* which translates roughly as "Never tickle a sleeping dragon."[7]

Lewis's dragons are watchful and Rowling's are sleeping, but there is a connection in not disturbing or drawing the attention of the dangerous serpent within readers (note the consistency of this image with Harry's internal serpent in both *Order of the Phoenix* and *Half-Blood Prince*). Certainly in writing magical fantasy stories laden with spiritual meaning and images, Rowling follows Lewis and Tolkien's lead—and shares in their success. The "old man" in us is naturally defensive against edifying Christian messages. The Harry Potter books lower these defenses because they're wrapped in a children's story, as well as—I have to say—in stories that so many Christians have said lack Christian meaning! Like a judo master who throws his opponent by taking advantage of the opponent's aggression, the Harry Potter books have been able to deliver their message the world over. Because of the ironic—if well-intentioned—objections of many, this message of faith comes wrapped in a package marked "not for Christians," and is reaching those most resistant to Christian belief.

WHAT HAS TO HAPPEN IN THE REMAINING HARRY POTTER BOOK

Part of the fun of realizing the formula in each book is that it encourages us to imagine what the end of the Harry Potter epic "must" be. Let me confess to you that I have made my share of predictions, and outside of the alchemy-related guesses for *Half-Blood Prince* (that Dumbledore would die, that it would be the cold and moist "white" work, and that Severus Snape was the Half-Blood Prince), if you don't know my other predictions, I hope you never find out just how badly I have fared at the divinations game! Having said that, let me say what we *can* expect to happen in the saga's finale, with respect to Rowling's alchemical artistry, narrative misdirection, and thematic conclusions.

Alchemy

I will call the last book, whose title at this writing has not been announced, *Harry Potter and the Alchemist's Cell*, both because it is one of the titles Warner Brothers has copyrighted for use in future movies and computer games and because I want to emphasize the alchemical nature of the finale. Harry Potter and the "Great Work" of alchemy are seven-stage processes, and we should have a "philosophical child" or "philosopher's stone" at the end of each, if the Work is successful.

Order of the Phoenix was the nigredo, or black stage, of alchemy, and *Half-Blood Prince* was the albedo, or white stage. *Alchemist's Cell*, if the pattern continues to the end as we should expect, should be the rubedo, or red stage. There are three things we can expect in the rubedo: the resolution of contraries, the chemical wedding, and the production of the stone. Rowling has carefully prepared us for all three in *Half-Blood Prince.*

Because Sirius Black died at the end of the black stage and Albus Dumbledore died at the end of the white stage, the big question left is this: Will Hagrid, whose name means red (Sirius Black means black, and Albus Dumbledore means white), have to die at the end of the red stage? He won't *have* to die, certainly, but I wouldn't bet against it. Other likely candidates include Rufus Scrimgeour, whose name means "the red man scrimmager," and all the redheaded Weasleys.

Most important of the reds, however, and nearest to Harry's heart, is Rubeus Hagrid. Hagrid is the first magical person Harry meets in his conscious life, the savior who rescues him from the Dursleys and reveals to him the magical world in which he belongs. Rubeus is a Dumbledore man through and through, by confession (remember his outrage when Vernon Dursley says an unkind word about the headmaster?), in deed (his inability to believe ill of Severus because Dumbledore trusted him), and by his sacrificial love for his unlovable brother, Grawp—a giant even their mother couldn't love—and the most horrible of magical creatures (dragons, acromantulas, and Blast-Ended Skrewts, to name a few). As a half giant, the beloved Keeper of Keys, I'm afraid, is a sure stand-in for the God-Man who sacrificed himself for us. This and his roguishly rouge name suggest that Hagrid won't survive *Alchemist's Cell.*

He doesn't *have* to die, though. Unlike Sirius Black and Albus Dumbledore, whose stages had to end in order to get through the alchemical work, Rubeus Hagrid as the physical embodiment of the third and last stage is actually the destination. And on top of that, Rowling is anything but mechanical in her use of alchemical imagery and is not bound to kill off characters just because of their names.

Hagrid's childlike innocence, his unconditional, sacrificial love for those despised by the world, and the symmetry of his death ending Tom Riddle's nightmare existence (by destroying the trophy Horcrux Riddle was given for "saving" Hogwarts from Hagrid's pet)—these things, as much as his name, make me worry for poor Hagrid.

More signs? Well, look for septenary deadlines: seven months, seven days, or seven hours counting down as the seven-year Great Work comes to a conclusion. I also suspect we might see a snake such as Nagini eating its tail (the uroboros is a symbol of the rotation of the elements), a man or a man and woman suspended on a wheel as a four-spoke axis (the turning of the great wheel), and a square resolved into a circle (the preferred image for this four-element-into-quintessence formula being a house described in these geometric terms, perhaps a domed building?).

These are rather esoteric possibilities of seven counting down to one, four being reduced to quintessential unity, and black and white becoming red and ending. The more expected possibilities of contraries being revealed and resolved and couples joining for death and birth are plot points we read about in *Half-Blood Prince*.

Alchemist's Cell will have to tie up the host of loose ends left hanging at the end of *Half-Blood Prince*. I expect a gaggle of revelations of secret Jekyll- and Hyde-like doppelgängers, beginning with Snape as a Dumbledore disciple (the alchemist in the title) and a half vampire, Draco as a werewolf, Horace Slughorn as a Death Eater, and Albus Dumbledore's last year as having been made possible by a "stoppered death" potion brewed by Snape. But these revelations, as extraordinary as they may seem, are not the end of the rubedo. It is the resolution of the contraries that is crucial.

The most important conflict this rubedo must resolve are the contraries of the central Gryffindor/Slytherin conflict in three generational rounds: Harry/Draco, Harry/Severus, and Harry/Tom Riddle Jr. Harry must also either overcome his internal prejudice before or during this work so that he can absorb or destroy the soul fragments in the four remaining Horcruxes, rally the four groups comprising the magical brethren, and unite the four Hogwarts houses for the battle with Voldemort and the Death Eaters. If Harry successfully resolves these quaternaries, he will have become the quintessence himself, a synonym in many alchemical texts for the philosopher's stone.

Curiously, the Philosopher's Stone is supposed to emerge during the rubedo from the white stone that appears at the end of the white work. A phoenix also should appear at the beginning of the rubedo.[8] Assuming that Dumbledore himself does not rise on the third day from the white tomb that appears magically at his funeral (the *Half-Blood Prince* story closes two days after his fall from the Tower), it seems Rowling is pointing to Harry as the successor to Dumbledore and probable "red stone." The repeated "I am with you" phrase and Harry's confessions to Scrimgeour of being a "Dumbledore man" signal, along with the phoenix Harry sees rising from the white tomb, that Harry will be the completion of Albus's work. Look for Fawkes to appear early in *Alchemist's Cell*.

We were signaled about the resolution of the fours into the quintessence in the sixth book, and we've wondered about how the Gryffindor/Slytherin chasm could be bridged since the beginning. I have to wonder, though, if the answer to all these things wasn't included with the chemical wedding announcements we were all sent in *Half-Blood Prince*. The wedding is the alchemical rotation and resolution of the four elements.

The contrary qualities of the four elements are likened to quarreling foes who must be reconciled or united in order for harmony to reign. The circulation of elements is identical with the process the alchemists describe as the conversion of body into spirit, and spirit into body, until each is able to mingle together, or unite in the chemical wedding to form a new perfect being, the philosopher's stone.[9]

The rubedo, as the final stage of the Great Work, features the wedding of the "red man" and "white woman" (often a king and queen), their copulation and death, and the birth of the orphan ("the philosophical child"). Burckhardt calls the chemical marriage the "central symbol of alchemy."[10] It has been the subject of literature, including Shakespeare's *Romeo and Juliet* (1595), John Donne's "The Extasie" (1607), Johann Andreae's *The Chymical Wedding of Christian Rosenkreutz* (1616), William Blake's "Jerusalem" (1804–1820), C. S. Lewis's *Perelandra* (1944) and *That Hideous Strength* (1946), and Lindsay Clarke's *The Chymical Wedding* (1989).

Let me spell out how Bill Weasley and Fleur Delacour conform to the red man and white woman of alchemy and what their wedding may mean in *Alchemist's Cell*. Both Bill and Fleur are cartoons or caricatures of a studly man and a drop-dead beautiful woman. When Bill is bit by a werewolf, he risks becoming in fact only the macho image he has projected to the world for some time (remember his long hair and fang earrings?). Fleur's hypnotic beauty and enchanting kisses are both signs that she is an almost allegorical figure for feminine allure and magic. Red-haired Bill is a machismo kind of guy with a werewolf lurking below the surface (one step up from the already-fiery weasel), and Fleur is the fashion model, a wild white woman whose talons, cruel beak, and scaly wings are also just out of sight.

Ginny is right on too, I think, when she says that Bill is interested in Fleur because he "likes a bit of adventure."[11] Fire and water are opposites that attract, even though they are a combination that resolve the qualities of both. Fleur, the silver-haired super-feminine beauty featured in *Half-Blood Prince*, is a cold and wet sign of the white work that features the water element after the torching experience of *Phoenix*. However, when we see Fleur become angry and aggressive over the passive body of Bill, who was bested by Greyback at the end of *Half-Blood Prince*, we know that she has become sufficiently masculine or choleric to move the choleric Mrs. Weasley to a more feminine and passive state. The chemical wedding at the end of the rotation of the elements, when water becomes fiery and fire, liquid or passive, is in full progress.

As any student of *Romeo and Juliet* (or *West Side Story*) will tell you, although the chemical wedding of opposites may mean great things for the citizens of Verona, as the Capulets and Montagues reconcile over the dead bodies of the honeymooners, it's not a marriage that parents desire for their children. The fact that the new king and queen, archetypes of masculine fire and feminine water, die soon after their marriage reflects the end and goal of the alchemical work.

According to alchemical theory, generation cannot take place unless there has first been a death. In Christian mysticism, the same idea occurs with the parable of the grain of wheat that must first die in the earth before it can bring forth fruit (see John 12:24-25), a parable that alchemists often cite. The philosopher's stone cannot be generated until the lovers have died and their bodies putrefied in the mercurial waters.[12]

I imagine this sounds perfectly dreadful to you, especially if you're thinking it means Bill and Fleur's wedding day will be a bloodbath. It needn't be (I'll explain why in a minute), but even if it is, these deaths—be they literal or figurative—will bring forth life.

Closely related to the symbolism of marriage is that of death.

This connection between marriage and death as part of the nature of things is indicated by the fact that, according to ancient experience, marriage in a dream means a death, and a death in a dream means a marriage. This correspondence is based on the idea that any given union presupposes an extinction of the earlier state. In the marriage of a man and a woman, each gives up part of his or her independence, whereas death (which is in the first instance a separation) is followed by the union of the body with the earth and the soul with its original essence.[13]

The child born of the coition of this death to self and opening to the spirit is the "philosophical child" or "philosopher's stone," also known, for obvious reasons, as "the orphan."

The Philosopher's Stone Is Produced

I have to think you might be asking, "So, you're saying Bill and Fleur will die at their wedding or soon after *and* that a child will be born miraculously from their brief marriage *and* that this child will be the answer to death or at least Lord Voldemort? What do you take me for?" There is a reasonable answer to this understandable skepticism!

Let me say again that alchemy doesn't force plot turns. The real master alchemist, J. K. Rowling, is certainly obeying the rules of alchemical drama, but she does so in conformity to the tradition of telling the tale as it needs to be told.

What I mean by this is that Bill and Fleur don't *have* to die physical deaths. The couples joined by chemical marriages in Lewis's Space Trilogy, for instance, don't die except in the Elizabethan usage of that term. It could very well be that the death Bill and Fleur die is in the "extinction of their earlier, still differentiated state" of fire and water. This rotation of the elements can be a physical death, of course. But it can also mean the death to self:

in Fleur's case, phlegmatic excess and selfishness (seen in righteous anger with her mother-in-law to be) and in the Weasleys' case to choleric British pride and machismo (seen in Bill's passivity in the hospital bed and Molly's surrender to and embracing her daughter-in-law with the offer of a family heirloom to highlight her silver hair). This death has already happened and is the accomplishment of the alchemical wedding—which death and wedding promise a new life to celebrate at book's end.

The production of the philosopher's stone, then, is well under way by the end of *Half-Blood Prince.* We have seen the preface to the chemical wedding, and we have been shown the various quaternaries and contraries that need to be revealed and resolved in this finale to the seven-stage alchemical work. The seven will become one, the various fours will become or unite behind the quintessence, and the twos—especially the Gryffindor/Slytherin split between Harry and Draco, Harry and Severus, and Harry and Lord Voldemort but also all the doppelgängers, the contrary pairs, even the twins (if Fred and George die heroically as I suspect they will)—will come into the light of day and find resolution and peace. Either Harry will become the philosopher's stone he is destined to become by overcoming his prejudice and becoming a vehicle of love, or the bad guys will triumph.

As it is, the Harry Potter books are a gift to the world and especially to the Christian community, a gift that should be celebrated from the housetops. We live in a world of demeaning entertainments and distracting "goodies" that divert our attention from the essentials and diminish our capacity to focus on the means to cheat death. Into this world comes Harry Potter, a delightful story overflowing with magic and laughter as well as images and meaningful stories that foster our greater life in Christ. Joining in Harry's adventures in our imaginations, we are trained in the "stock responses," conditioned to make the hard, right choices for the good, and taught to look to Love himself as the answer to a world enamored of sin and death.

I do not know the details of Rowling's religious confession besides what is reported in our Muggle media, namely, that she is a member of the Church of Scotland and that she says her faith is key to understanding the books.[14] I am grateful to her, whatever her intentions or religious beliefs may really be, for the boon she has offered to the world through the Harry Potter novels.

I close by repeating the response C. S. Lewis made to Christian critics who objected to the magic in his Narnia series:

Do you think I am trying to weave a spell? Perhaps I am; but remember your fairy tales. Spells are used for breaking enchantments as well as inducing them. And you and I have need of the strongest spell that can be found to wake us from the evil enchantment of worldliness which has been laid upon us for nearly a hundred years.[15]

We still have a need for counterspells—enchantments to do battle with our profane worldview—stronger and perhaps more dangerous spells and magic than were warranted in Lewis's day. But that's all the more reason to celebrate the success of Harry Potter. This series is a small light shining in a much-darkened world. It is a small light but a brilliant one, a light that will not be comprehended by the darkness because it is a reflection of the Life that came into the world as the "light of men" (John 1:4). Three cheers for Harry Potter and for his greatest magic—the baptism of the world's imagination!

SPEAKING OF GOD
IN HARRY POTTER

When I speak at churches and bookstores, I am always asked at least once, either during the question time after the talk or in a private moment later, about how to share the meaning of Harry Potter with children. I can certainly understand the concern; as a daddy of seven and a homeschooler, I struggle to keep up with what my children are reading and thinking—and to keep them on course with biblical values and virtue. In this section, I want to share with you some thoughts about how I have used Harry Potter in teaching and connecting with my own children (everyone but the three-year-old!).

Before I start, though, let me say that I've never met a kid who wants to be told by an adult the meaning of Harry Potter without some proof that you know what you're talking about. How are they to know you aren't on a "parent/adult power trip thing" (as a Barnes and Noble University student sagely told me)? Whether your children have the Harry Potter books memorized or simply know that all their friends like the books, in order to have a meaningful conversation, you'll need to demonstrate that you take this seriously because it's important to them. And you have to know more about Harry than what you can read about in the newspapers or pick up at a church coffee hour.

I recommend that you use Harry to talk about subjects that are important to you and your family. To make good use of Harry, though, isn't as easy as just deciding to do it. Like everything else worth doing, it will take some effort to do it right. When you build a house, you start with the blueprints, then you lay the foundation, and finally, you build the building according to the plan. Using Harry to teach your children is no different: first you'll need to map out what you want to use Harry to do, then you'll lay your foundation carefully, and finally, you'll follow through on your mapped-out objectives.

MAP OUT A PLAN

Before you can begin to use Harry in teaching your children, it's important at the start that you have your goals, whatever they are, clearly in mind. Time management gurus are right when they tell us to "begin with the end in mind." Figure out where you want to wind up before you head out the door to begin the journey. The same is true with these books. I speak with parents on both sides of the Harry Potter issue. Some have embraced the books and rejoice that their children have found Harry to be a worthy read. Others are unsure about the books and have avoided everything to do with Potter-mania. But regardless of which side of the fence parents land on, most of them seem to have the same goals when it comes to raising their kids. Both groups want to talk to their children about the difference between good and bad books, what the Bible tells us about sorcery and magic, and how Harry Potter fits into these ideas. The Harry Potter books are wonderfully suited to these goals.

When it comes to Harry Potter, what are your goals? Do you hope the books will encourage your child's love of reading great literature? Do you plan to use the books to start a conversation about love and sacrifice? Maybe you simply want to protect your kids against the occult and New Age propaganda.

Once you decide what it is you want to teach with Harry Potter, you're ready to move to the next step: laying the foundation.

LAY THE FOUNDATION

When it comes to teaching our kids, the mistake people make is not usually in the planning. We parents are only too clear about where we want to go and what we want the children to under-stand—NOW! The problem comes when we jump from our plan-ning to the finishing work on the roof and interior before we have laid the foundation or put up the walls.

For parents who want to introduce their child to Harry and for those whose child may live at Hogwarts 24/7 via his internal "imagination station," the procedure is the same. Planning first, foundation second. Emperor Augustus's maxim is still good advice today: *festina lente*, or "make haste slowly." Build a strong founda-tion to speak from, and you will be able to reach your goals. If you skip this step, expect to be ignored or dismissed.

First in importance, then, is the how-to of laying the foundation. I read the first four books to five of my children; it was one of the best times we have had reading together as a family. I cannot rec-ommend this enough. Even if you and your kids have read the books once, please believe me, they are worth reading aloud. They are not lyrical poetry, certainly; they're more like play scripts, which means they're improved by public performance.

Why bother? This is a big deal to children, especially if you don't read aloud often. Reading aloud gives your children the opportunity to share the story with you while experiencing it with their ears rather than their eyes—which is as different from reading as a radio broadcast or movie, truth be told.[1] The fact that Mom and Dad are doing it makes it that much more special. Reading aloud is a foundation, too, that makes possible two types of conversation.

Nine out of ten conversations I have with children (mine and others) about Harry Potter are *not* "teaching conversations." This first type of conversation is simply the discussion of what is happening in the story as they read it or as they reflect on it later: "Who put Harry's name in the Goblet?" "Why does Draco hate Harry so much?" "Can they win the Quidditch Cup this year?" "How do they get past Fluffy?" Believe me, your children will be thrilled to talk with you about what they think—and to refute your silly answers to these questions.

While I am the Harry guru on my block and an authority when I speak in public, it's a rare-bird child who asks me "What's it all about, Mr. Granger?" What I get more often is a question about something that really concerns them, engaged as they are with the stories and the characters. "Are Ron and Hermione dating now?" "Will they get married in the last book?" "My friend Jack tells me that Snape really didn't kill Dumbledore and that the headmaster is still alive. Is he crazy or what?" "Why didn't Dumbledore just tell Harry about the prophecy at the *beginning* of *Phoenix?*"

They ask me these questions or I ask them similar ones. Not only is this great for reviewing the books in your head or with the books in hand, it really gets your kids to think and to accept you as a fellow reader. These conversations are a lot of fun—especially if you suggest what you think will happen in the coming books. When I used to say (as I did at every talk for several years) that

Dumbledore had to die at the end of the sixth book, I knew the room would split into two camps: those who thought the idea was preposterous and those who would argue my side.

Maybe you don't have time to read Harry aloud to your kids, or maybe your kids are in their teens and won't let you. Maybe you've hated reading aloud since your brothers teased you about it when you were learning to read (not uncommon!). Don't worry. Reading aloud is not the only way to connect with your kids. Another way to lay the foundation to talk about Harry is by buying the tapes. Not only are they very well done—the British comedian who reads them is outstanding—but you can play them in the car or while you're washing the dishes. I didn't really understand the depth of the Harry Potter books until after I listened to the books on tape when we took a family trip from Houston to the Olympic Peninsula of Washington (where we live now). Listening together on car rides or at home may even be better than reading aloud because you get to do exactly what your kids are doing: listen and think about the story!

Once you've read the book (or all the books), and often even before, you'll find that your questions can move from "What happened in the story?" to "What (and whom) do you like and dislike in Harry Potter?" While talking about events, motivations, and why a character didn't do what you thought they might, if your children are like my children, you will now hear about which characters they like and which ones they don't like.

This isn't a small point. It's a turning point. Child psychologists now use Harry as a Rorschach test of sorts with young patients; to find out more about them, they ask children which characters they like or what their favorite parts of the books are. Interestingly enough, psychologists who work with very disturbed children report even children with horrible backgrounds and problems almost without exception are normal in that they love Harry and hate Voldemort.[2] Discussions about which Harry Potter characters are good, which ones are bad, and which ones we can't be sure about—and why—can open the door to important discussions about everything meaningful in Harry Potter. Please don't expect your children to listen to you explain the formulas of the books or talk about the meaning behind the symbolism of the phoenix until you've shared which characters you like in the books and what you like (and don't like) about them. This conversation, especially when you've listened to your children's likes and dislikes, demonstrates that you share their concerns—which, until they're twenty-five years old at least (if not forever), will be largely about wanting to be liked (or disliked for the right reasons!).

Once this door is open, you can drive a truck through it. Take the time to build this foundation by listening to tapes, reading the books with your kids or by yourself, and talking with your kids about the stories. Once you have established yourself as a Harry reader (even if you are like my wife's aunt, who hates fantasy fiction), then you can move on to the next steps of conversation.

BUILD THE HOUSE

Level two of Harry Potter conversations with your children depends largely on your goals. For many families, the main concern is to ensure that their child is immunized against occult behaviors and that he or she knows the biblical injunctions against sorcery and the real-world dangers of New Age philosophy and cult groups. Other parents want to use Harry both to teach these lessons and to teach their children to love good books. Both goals are easily reached using a child's love of these stories. *Looking for God in Harry Potter* is more about the meaning of Harry Potter in light of Christian faith than it is about Harry's roots in English literature, so I'll focus on the goal of teaching the dangers of the occult. My children love to pretend that they are characters in Harry Potter (my oldest daughter even has a hand-turned wand I was given by the WhirlWood master craftsman). The younger ones run around the house with rulers and sticks for wands, towels tied around their necks for capes, and newspaper twisted into cone-shaped hats. Playtime in our yard is something of a magical Olympic Games and medieval tournament combined (we read many of Howard Pyle's King Arthur books, too). The boys blast each other with spells, and the girls try to sneak up on their less clever (or deceitful?) brothers. I think by now my neighbors know what *Expelliarmus* and *Tarantallegra* mean (or at least what's supposed to happen to you when you're hit with these spells). My children clearly think magic is a lot of fun and one stage on which they can act out a variety of roles: good guys, bad guys, champion, victim, avenger, hostage, etc.

As a parent, the concern I have is that my children will think all magic is fun and will be susceptible to seduction by the real-world dangers of occult groups. This is not paranoia. However, there has not been a "huge upswing" or even growth in the occult since the Harry Potter books appeared, as the Harry haters have claimed. What has happened, if only because of the controversy created by well-intentioned but misinformed Christians, is that there has been a link created between Harry Potter and the occult. These groups, though they know the magic of Harry Potter has nothing to do with sorcery or nature worship, have shamelessly exploited this link by creating mock Hogwarts-type Web sites to draw in young Harry fans who are surfing the Internet to learn more about magic.

Being concerned about these things, then, is not parental micromanagement but simple prudence and an awareness of New Age groups, their beliefs, and the distance of these beliefs from Christian orthodoxy. It's also the knowledge that the reason Scripture forbids sorcery is because it is a danger to individuals and their communities. So how do we share this with kids who are having a good time playing witches and wizards?

Easy, really. Ask any child if he or she thinks the magic in Harry Potter and their games is real. When asked this question, my children will all look at you with that special gaze of disdain reserved for patronizing adults ("I was born at night, Dad, but not *last* night"). Younger children might blur the worlds between fiction and reality (because their whole world is still magical and all about discovery—you press a button and the car radio turns on—it's magic!). But children older than seven or eight years old usually have the pretend/real boundaries pretty clear in their head.

Your job is to mess up these boundaries again. Explain to them that there is real-world magic and tell them its real-world names: sorcery, wicca, nature worship, etc. Believe me, they'll probably be astonished and probably incredulous. Assure them you're not kidding! When they ask where they can go to sign up for Hogwarts training, you can then explain the difference between the pretend magic of Harry Potter and the real-world dangers of the New Age and the occult.

In a nutshell, the difference that children can understand is this: Pretend magic comes from within, and real-world magic comes from outside. The "inside" kind of magic is a story-picture of our relationship with God and the miracles that happen when the kingdom of heaven is alive in our heart. This is a good kind of magic and exists only in stories; just as God says his Word and creates the world every moment, so Harry Potter characters say the magic words and magic happens. Point out that you understand they know this doesn't work when they wave their wands, although it is a lot of fun to play Merlin and Harry games and read the books.

Real-world wizards, in contrast, don't work from the inside but instead do their magic by calling in outside help. This magic depends on two things: help from demons and believing that you can control what these demons will do. I contrast this with prayers we say as a family. When we pray, we ask for help from God and surrender our will to his, trusting in his love and mercy. Magicians don't do this; they ask for help from demons and think they know enough to control or limit what the demons do in their life.

I tell my kids this is a little like playing on a busy street and thinking you can "control" the traffic. Demons, like drivers, have their own ideas—and unlike the drivers, these dark powers want to hurt you and only lack access to your heart to do their damage. I tell them stories of childhood friends who have lost their way into occult practice through games like Dungeons and Dragons, astrology, tarot, even natural food diets, when they take the step from pretend and fun to opening their heart to demons.

If your children understand Scripture as more than just arbitrary rules, that is, if they know the Bible is a lifesaving guidebook or "owner's manual" for how human beings should live their lives, you can then share with them the biblical warnings against sorcery. Explain that God tells us this to protect us from the fallen angels who want to keep us from our hope of eternal life with him. If your children are old enough, you can detail the difference between the psychic and spiritual realms we discussed in chapter 1 of this book. For teens, I've found this distinction is a real help.

This is important stuff. And I have to say it again: This talk is a conversation that grows out of your having read enough Harry Potter to have been accepted as a fellow reader. Maybe your parenting style is the Mount Sinai type, where you deliver the commandments from on high and your children toe the line unquestioningly. If that works for you, congratulations! My children and their friends require a more sympathetic and at-their-level approach.

These real-world magic talks in my family, consequently, can happen anywhere: on drives in the car, at the dinner table, or on walks and runs when we're talking about the stories. It is not forced or done lecture-style but grows out of their love for the stories and the love I have for my kids. When you read the Harry Potter books, you show your children that you care about what is important to them. Because of this, their hearts will be open to your expertise in these matters and they will take your message seriously.

After I explain the "big picture" to my children, I can then draw parallels between the Harry Potter stories and our lives as Christians. This should be obvious to them, really. That the battle between Gryffindor and Slytherin is a story version of our real battle with Satan; that Harry's external and internal battles with the Dark Lord are just like our own need to resist the devil, who exists as an evil personage outside of us and inside of us as much as we allow him (a good time to talk about what Harry's occlumency and our own watchfulness over our heart have in common!). That the answer to sin and death in our life, just like in Harry Potter, is love and faith.

Here, of course, is where understanding the books (their formulas, themes, symbolism, even the names) as I have explained it in this book helps a bunch. Your child is probably aware that other Christians think these books are dangerous, even evil—and now you're saying they're *good books* and about life in Christ? Knowing your stuff here, even if only being able to explain how Harry dies at the end of every book and rises from the dead as we hope to, seals their trust in you and their grasp of the difference between pretend magic and occult danger.

These conversations about the meaning of Harry Potter can

eventually shape your child's understanding of the place books and entertainment should properly have in our lives. Ask your children what they thought or felt when they read the graveyard scene in *Goblet of Fire* or when Harry returns to the Dursleys every year. As you listen to their responses to story events and share your own, you'll be able to draw the connections between the stories and God's design for us to have a life in him. The thrill of Harry Potter is the thrill of realizing that there is a reality behind the images in the stained glass windows at church—that something is shining through these stories and that our lives are incomplete without it.

If you invest yourself in your children's future by reading what they read, they will be able to learn from you that Harry Potter is a great story because it is an echo of the Great Story of God becoming man, the real-world Story that saves us. You can share with them that all great stories echo the Great Story of God and that this is why you encourage them to read good books. Reading books that support and point to our faith is like learning to add before you multiply and eating well even when you're not sick. The imagination, like every part of us, needs to be brought into God's service. Books like Harry Potter help to baptize and shape the imagination.

I don't doubt that you and I (and every parent) do this sharing differently. Some of my friends think that every time Harry and his friends bend rules or lie to teachers is a great failing. I tell my children that just like us, these characters make mistakes, but then we also talk about how the deception is usually done in an attempt to thwart evil. Having read *Tom Brown's Schooldays*, the model of English boarding school books and Christian fiction, and knowing what I do about the structures and meaning of Harry Potter, I understand that this genre *requires* misbehavior in the first years of the story. Without it, the transformation to virtue and decision to do good in the end would mean nothing.

But however individual families may differ in their approach and understanding, I commend these stories to you as you "train up a child in the way he should go" (Proverbs 22:6, KJV). I believe the books are a providential help to parents in these end times to win the hearts of our children for Christ and to support us in our walk as individuals and as families. Thank you in advance for what good use you make of this book toward this goal and for writing me at john@hogwartsprofessor.com with your thoughts, questions, and success stories. I look forward to hearing from you!

John, asking your prayers

ENDNOTES

INTRODUCTION

1 See http://www.the-leaky-cauldron.org/quickquotes/articles/1998/0798-telegraph-bertodano.html.

2 See http://www.quick-quote-quill.org/articles/1999/0099-amazon-staff.htm.

3 See http://www.quick-quote-quill.org/articles/2000/1000-vancouversun-wyman.htm.

CHAPTER 1

1 For more on the confusion between the psychic and the spiritual realms in our time and the dangers of occultism, please see Charles Upton's *The System of Antichrist: Truth and Falsehood in Postmodernism and the New Age* (Ghent, NY: Sophia Perennis, 2001), 134–137.

2 See C. S. Lewis, *Prince Caspian*, chapters 7 and 12. Readers of the Narnia books remember from *The Magician's Nephew* that Aslan created that world with his song—as does the divinity in J. R. R. Tolkien's Middle Earth.

3 C. S. Lewis, *Mere Christianity* (New York: Collier Books, 1960), 51.

4 "Fundamentalism Afoot in Anti-Potter Camp, Says New-Religions Expert: Popular Culture Enjoys an Autonomy, Explains Massimo Introvigne," *Zenit News*, December 6, 2001, http://www.cesnur.org/2001/potter/dec _03.htms.

5 Bishop Auxentios, *Orthodox Tradition* 20, no. 3 (2003): 14–26.

6 See C. S. Lewis's *The Silver Chair* for this modern tragedy told in story form. *The Silver Chair* is a vibrant story of the confusion and modern enchantment with materialism or "life underground." Is there any Narnia moment greater than Prince Rilian's victory over the Emerald Witch in chapter 12?

CHAPTER 2

1 Tom Shippey, *J. R. R. Tolkien: Author of the Century* (Boston: Houghton Mifflin Co., 2001), 147.

2 Perry Glazer, "The Surprising Trouble with Harry," *Touchstone* (November 2003): 13.

CHAPTER 3

1 David Colbert, author of *The Magical Worlds of Harry Potter*, thinks the formula is the Universal Hero pattern described by Joseph Campbell in his *Hero with a Thousand Faces*. Joan Acocella in the *New Yorker* magazine traces the pattern to Vladimir Propp's 1929 book, *Morphology of the Folk Tale*. Elizabeth Schafer believes Rowling is a fan of Carl Jung; she cites Lord Ragland's work on archetypal heroes, *The Hero: A Study in Tradition, Myth, and Drama*, as a guide to the formula Rowling follows.

CHAPTER 4

[1] For more information on alchemy and its use in classic literature, please read *Darke Hierogliphicks* by Stanton Linden, a history of alchemy and its usage in English literature, or subscribe to *Cauda Pavonis*, an academic journal on alchemy in literature.

[2] *The Tempest, Romeo and Juliet, Antony and Cleopatra, The Two Gentlemen of Verona, The Comedy of Errors, Love's Labours Lost,* and *The Merchant of Venice* come to mind. In her book *The Art of Memory* (Chicago: University of Chicago Press, 1974), Dame Frances Yates demonstrated that Shakespeare built the Globe Theatre on alchemical principles for the proper staging of his alchemical dramas.

[3] Lyndy Abraham, *A Dictionary of Alchemical Imagery* (Cambridge: Cambridge University Press, 1999).

[4] Ibid.

[5] Ibid.

[6] Ibid.

[7] Mircea Eliade and Stepehn Corrin, *The Forge and the Crucible: The Origins and Structures of Alchemy* (Chicago: University of Chicago Press, 1979), 153.

[8] In alchemical lore, frequently a copulating couple are buried and die, but in their death, their spirits are joined and the Hermaphrodite body rises from the grave. This is the alchemical ending of *Romeo and Juliet* and why their deaths resolve their families' feud.

CHAPTER 5

[1] For more on this, see the discussion of the spell in chapter 13 on *Prisoner of Azkaban*.

[2] J. K. Rowling, *Harry Potter and the Order of the Phoenix* (New York: Scholastic, 2003), 27.

[3] Ibid., chapter 37.

[4] J. K. Rowling, *Harry Potter and the Half-Blood Prince* (New York: Scholastic, 2005), 511.

CHAPTER 6

[1] See "Why *Half-Blood Prince* Is the Best Harry Potter Novel" at http://www.HogwartsProfessor.com.

CHAPTER 7

[1] Malcolm Jones, "Harry's Hot," *Newsweek* (July 17, 2000): 56.

[2] J. K. Rowling, *Harry Potter and the Sorcerer's Stone* (New York: Scholastic, 1997), chapter 17.

[3] Ibid., chapter 17.

[4] J. K. Rowling, *Harry Potter and the Prisoner of Azkaban* (New York: Scholastic, 1999), 427–428.

[5] See "But Obviously Dumbledore Is Not Jesus" and "Why *Half-Blood Prince* Is the Best Harry Potter Novel," both at http://www.HogwartsProfessor.com.

6 Rowling, *Order of the Phoenix*, chapter 38.

7 Ibid., chapter 34.

8 J. K. Rowling, *Harry Potter and the Goblet of Fire* (New York: Scholastic, 2000), chapter 33.

9 Rowling, *Order of the Phoenix*, chapter 36.

10 Rowling, *Prisoner of Azkaban*, chapter 12.

11 Rowling, *Order of the Phoenix*, chapter 37.

12 Ibid., chapter 37.

13 Ibid., chapter 36.

14 Ibid., chapter 37.

15 Rowling, *Sorcerer's Stone*, chapter 17.

CHAPTER 8

1 See Aristotle's *Nicomachean Ethics*, book 2, for the longer definition.

2 Rowling, *Goblet of Fire*, 36.

3 Ibid., 37.

4 Rowling, *Sorcerer's Stone*, 6, and *Goblet of Fire*, 37.

5 J. K. Rowling, *Harry Potter and the Chamber of Secrets* (New York: Scholastic, 1999), chapter 11.

6 Rowling, *Sorcerer's Stone*, 59.

7 Rowling, *Prisoner of Azkaban*, 21.

8 Rowling, *Goblet of Fire*, 31.

9 Rowling, *Order of the Phoenix*, 2.

10 Rowling, *Chamber of Secrets*, 18.

11 Ibid., 17.

12 Rowling, *Half-Blood Prince*, 512.

13 See http://www.mugglenet.com/jkrinterview.shtml.

CHAPTER 9

1 Martin Lings, *Symbol and Archetype: A Study of the Meaning of Existence* (Cambridge: Quinta Essentia), vii.

2 Bishop Auxentios, "The Iconic and Symbolic in Orthodox Iconography," *Orthodox Tradition* 4, no. 3 (n.d.): 49–64. See also http://www.orthodoxinfo.com/general/orth_icon.htm.

3 The symbolism springs from Plato's myth of the charioteer in the *Phaedrus* (246b, 254c-e) and its explanation in the *Republic* (441e–442b). The disciples of the apostles and of Christ "baptized" this doctrine in light of the Christian revelation in the first centuries AD.

4 C. S. Lewis, *Abolition of Man* (New York: Collier Books), 28.

[5] Rowling, *Chamber of Secrets*, 11.

[6] J. K. Rowling, *Fantastic Beasts and Where to Find Them* (n.p.: Bt Bound, 2001), 20.

[7] David Colbert, *The Magical Worlds of Harry Potter: A Treasury of Myths, Legends, and Fascinating Facts* (n.p.: Bt Bound, 2002), 107.

[8] Rowling, *Chamber of Secrets*, 18.

[9] Colbert, *Magical Worlds*, 109.

[10] Rowling, *Sorcerer's Stone*, chapters 14–15.

[11] Rowling, *Goblet of Fire*, chapter 24.

[12] *Strong's Concordance of the Bible*, s.v. "unicorn."

[13] Colbert, *Magical Worlds*, 182.

[14] J. E. Cirlot notes that Carl Jung mentioned this symbolism with a reference to an author contemporaneous with the tapestries: "The very fierce animal with one horn is called unicorn. In order to catch it, a virgin is put in a field; the animal then comes to her and is caught, because it lies down in her lap. *Christ is represented by this animal, and his invincible strength by its horn.* He who lay down in the womb of the virgin has been caught by the hunters; that is to say, he was found in human shape by those who loved him." "Honoris of Autun, Speculum de Mysteriis Ecclesiae (Eyeglass of the Mysteries of the Church)," quoted in *Symbolism*, 357–358; emphasis mine. Not convinced? Paul Ford in his encyclopedic *Companion to Narnia* confirmed my memory and this interpretation. The unicorn, he reports, is "a mythological beast with a single horn in the center of its head. It variously symbolizes purity, chastity, and even *the Word of God as brought by Jesus Christ* " (emphasis mine). See Paul Ford, *Companion to Narnia* (San Francisco: HarperSanFrancisco, 1994), 430.

[15] J. E. Cirlot, *A Dictionary of Symbols* (New York: Dorset Press, 1991), 254; Allan Kronzek and Elizabeth Kronzek, *The Sorcerer's Companion* (New York: Broadway Books, 2001), 188; Colbert, *Magical Worlds*, 82.

[16] Rowling, *Prisoner of Azkaban*, chapter 22.

[17] Ford, *Companion to Narnia*, 440.

[18] See Cirlot, *Dictionary of Symbols*, 308–309. "Its symbolic meaning is linked with that of the tree of life . . . inexhaustible life, and is therefore equivalent to a symbol of immortality . . . because of the resemblance of its antlers to branches. It is also a symbol of the cycles of regeneration and growth. . . . The stag . . . came to be thought of as a symbol of regeneration because of the way its antlers are renewed. Like the eagle and the lion, it is the secular enemy of the serpent . . . [and acts] as [one of the] mediators of heaven and earth. . . . In the West, during the Middle Ages, the way of solitude and purity was often symbolized by the stag, which actually appears in some emblems with a crucifix between its horns."

[19] Rowling, *Prisoner of Azkaban*, chapter 20.

[20] Ford, *Companion to Narnia*, 358.

21 C. S. Lewis, *The Last Battle* (New York: Collier Books, 1960), 193.

22 Lewis didn't see the horse, the centaur's driving part, as a passionate creature, but as the desires (or belly) in alignment and in service to will and spirit (chest and head), especially when hosting a human rider. The centaur, "a semi-divine being with the head and chest of a man and the body of a horse," the embodiment of horse and rider, represents the reconciliation "of our spiritual and physical nature." "For Lewis, the Centaur represents the harmony of nature and spirit." See Ford, *Companion to Narnia*, 102, 235.

23 For the full story, see Colbert, *Magical Worlds*, 113–116.

24 Allan Zola Kronzek and Elizabeth Kronzek, *The Sorcerer's Companion: A Guide to the Magical World of Harry Potter* (n.p.: Bt Bound, 2001), 109.

25 Cirlot, *A Dictionary of Symbols*, 149.

26 Titus Burckhardt, *Alchemy: Science of the Cosmos, Science of the Soul* (Baltimore: Penguin Books, 1972), 18.

27 C. S. Lewis, *The Lion, the Witch and the Wardrobe* (New York: Collier Books, 1970), 104.

28 Burckhardt, *Alchemy*, 91.

29 Rowling, *Sorcerer's Stone*.

30 See "But Obviously Dumbledore Is Not Jesus" at http://www.Hogwarts Professor.com.

31 This is how C. S. Lewis described the effect that the works of George MacDonald had on him. See *George MacDonald: 365 Readings* (New York: Macmillan Publishing, 1986), xvi.

CHAPTER 10

1 Donna Farley, private correspondence.

2 For more on Helena Blavatsky, see *The Theosophical Enlightenment* by Joscelyn Godwin (Albany, N.Y.: The State University of New York Press, 1994). This book is a remarkable introduction to a woman whose wild ideas still, alas, influence our world.

3 Francis Bridger, *A Charmed Life: The Spirituality of Potterworld* (n.p.: Image Books, 2002), 19.

4 Linda McCabe, private correspondence.

5 Rowling, *Chamber of Secrets*, 3.

6 See http://ww2.netnitco.net/users/legend01/weasel.htm.

7 Rowling, *Prisoner of Azkaban*, chapter 3.

8 A correspondent from Iceland, Sigurdur Arni Thordarson, taught me that lilies are held by the archangel Gabriel at the Annunciation in Western iconography; the dead hold the lilies like Gabriel in anticipation of Christ's coming again to earth.

9 When *Book* magazine, a publication of Barnes and Noble, featured a mug shot of Rowling on their June 2003 cover to herald the arrival of *Harry Potter and the Order of the Phoenix*, they had no trouble finding five American men named Harry Potter, all of whom told the same tale of crank calls and new friends delighted to "meet the man himself." Rowling was sued in New Jersey by a children's book author whose story featured a

hero named Harry Potter. Better than these examples, Netflix released two mock-horror, B-movie gems, *Troll* (1986) and *Troll 2* (1992), in which the family resisting Torok the troll's attempt to take over the world is led by a dad and son both named Harry Potter. Harry Potter Sr. and Harry Potter Jr. were all over the movie and HBO screens for two or three years; how meaningful was that? (Not very.) Thanks to Dan Rees of Joplin, Missouri, for Harry's first encounters with trolls.

My favorite instance of Harry sightings pre-Rowling comes from Monty Python. In a send-up strangely echoing the beginning of *Sorcerer's Stone*, we hear Harry is about to be attacked: *It was a day like any other and Mr. and Mrs. Samuel Brainsample were a perfectly ordinary couple, leading perfectly ordinary lives—the sort of people to whom nothing extraordinary ever happened, and not the kind of people to be the centre of one of the most astounding incidents in the history of mankind. . . . So let's forget about them and follow instead the destiny of this man. . . . (Camera pans off them; they both look disappointed; camera picks up instead a smart little business man, in bowler, briefcase and pinstripes.) . . . Harold Potter, gardener, and tax official, first victim of Creatures from another Planet.* (See http://www.ibras.dk/montypython/episode07.htm. I learned of this early Python sketch from Kia, a friend of Linda McCabe's.)

[10] Saint Dorotheos, "On the Fear of God," *Dorotheos of Gaza* (Kalamazoo, Mich.: Cistercian Publications, 1977), 110–111.

CHAPTER 11

[1] Rowling, *Sorcerer's Stone*, chapter 15.

[2] Ibid., 258.

[3] See chapter 1 of Saint John Climacos, *The Ladder of Divine Ascent* (Mahwah, N.J.: Paulist Press, 1988).

[4] Rowling, *Sorcerer's Stone*, chapter 16.

[5] See Aristotle's *On the Soul;* William Wallace, *The Elements of Philosophy* (n.p.: Alba House, 1977), 62; and the relevant articles on "soul" in the *New Catholic Encyclopedia*.

[6] See Aristotle's *Nicomachean Ethics*, book 3, chapter 4.

[7] Rowling, *Sorcerer's Stone*, chapter 17.

[8] Ibid., chapter 16.

[9] Ibid., chapter 17.

[10] Alexandre Kalomiros, *River of Fire* (Montreal: Monastery Press, 1982), 18.

[11] Ioannes Romanides, *Franks, Romans, Feudalism, and Doctrine* (Brookline, Mass.: Holy Cross Orthodox Press, 1982), 46.

CHAPTER 12

[1] Rowling, *Chamber of Secrets*, chapter 18.

[2] Rowling has admitted that Lockhart has a real-world model. My guess is Philip Pullman, author of the Dark Materials trilogy. Certainly there are sufficient points

of correspondence between Pullman and Lockhart to merit serious consideration of the link: (1) as we know, Rowling likes to name characters in her books after characters from other famous books (see chapter 10), and one of the lead characters in multiple Pullman books is Sallie *Lockhart*; (2) Philip Pullman is a public atheist and despiser of organized religion—and admits freely in interviews that he proselytizes his worldview in his children's books; (3) Pullman is called the "UnLewis" in the UK because of his public disdain for C. S. Lewis's Narnia books and the values they represent.

CHAPTER 13
[1] Rowling, *Prisoner of Azkaban*, chapter 10.
[2] Ibid., chapter 12.
[3] Ibid., chapter 10.
[4] Ibid., chapter 12.
[5] Colbert, *Magical Worlds*, 125.
[6] Rowling, *Prisoner of Azkaban*, chapter 20.
[7] Ibid., chapter 19.
[8] Ibid., chapter 21.
[9] Ibid., chapter 21.

CHAPTER 14
[1] Thanks to Eileen Rebstock for her help in understanding the rebirthing party in *Goblet of Fire*.
[2] Rowling, *Fantastic Beasts*, 32.
[3] Rowling, *Sorcerer's Stone*, 294.
[4] Rowling, *Goblet of Fire*, chapter 16.

CHAPTER 15
[1] Rowling, *Order of the Phoenix*, chapter 38.
[2] Ibid.
[3] Abraham, *Alchemical Imagery*, 135.
[4] Ibid., 136.
[5] Rowling, *Order of the Phoenix*, chapters 37–38.
[6] Thanks to Dr. Amy Sturgis of Belmont University for pointing out the meaning of Moody's Disillusionment Charm.
[7] Rowling, *Order of the Phoenix*, chapter 37, *Half-Blood Prince*, chapter 28.
[8] Rowling, *Order of the Phoenix*, chapter 36.

CHAPTER 16
[1] Rowling, *Half-Blood Prince*, 513.

2 Ibid., 358.

3 Ibid., 511.

4 Ibid., 497.

5 Ibid., 498.

6 Compare to *Half-Blood Prince*, 511.

7 Ibid., 509.

8 Rowling, *Order of the Phoenix*, 733.

CHAPTER 17

1 Harold Bloom, "Harry and Hype," http://edition.cnn.com/2000/books/news/07/13/potter.hype; William Safire, "Besotted with Potter," *New York Times* (January 27, 2000); A. S. Bayatt, "Harry Potter and the Childish Adult," *New York Times* (July 1, 2003).

2 Suman Gupta, *Re-Reading Harry Potter* (New York: Palgrave Macmillan, 2003).

3 Gupta, *Re-Reading Harry Potter*; private correspondence from Alison Williams.

4 Huston Smith, *Why Religion Matters: The Fate of the Human Spirit in an Age of Disbelief* (San Francisco: HarperSanFrancisco, 2001), 120.

5 Mircea Eliade, *The Sacred and the Profane: The Nature of Religion* (New York: Harvest Books, 1968), 204–205.

6 C. S. Lewis, *Of Other Worlds* (New York: Collier Books, 1970), 37.

7 Thanks to Carrie Birmingham of Pepperdine for this insight.

8 Abraham, *A Dictionary of Alchemical Imagery*, 152.

9 Ibid., 138.

10 Ibid., 149.

11 Rowling, *Half-Blood Prince*, 93.

12 Abraham, *Dictionary of Alchemical Imagery*, 37.

13 Burckhardt, *Alchemy*, 156.

14 Quoted in Michael Nelson, "Fantasia: The Gospel according to C. S. Lewis," *The American Prospect* 13 no. 4 (February 25, 2002).

15 C. S. Lewis, *The Weight of Glory and Other Addresses* (New York: Collier, 1970), 7.

16 See http://www.HogwartsProfessor.com for much more discussion of the meaning of *Harry Potter and the Half-Blood Prince*.

APPENDIX

1 Jim Trelease, *The Read-Aloud Handbook: Why Parents Should Read Aloud*, 5th ed. (New York: Penguin, 2001).

2 Janet McConnaughey, "Harry Potter and the Shrinks," *AP* (May 8, 2001).